THE
COLLECTED
POEMS OF
F. R. SCOTT

OTHER BOOKS OF POETRY BY F.R. SCOTT

Overture (1945)
Events and Signals (1954)
The Eye of the Needle (1957)
St-Denys Garneau & Anne Hébert:
   Translations/Traductions (1962)
Signature (1964)
Selected Poems (1966)
Trouvailles (1967)
The Dance Is One (1973)
Poems of French Canada (trans.) (1977)

New Provinces (1936), edited with A.J.M. Smith
The Blasted Pine (1957; 2nd edition 1967), edited
   with A.J.M. Smith

Dialogue sur la traduction (1970), avec Anne Hébert

THE COLLECTED POEMS OF F. R. SCOTT

McCLELLAND AND STEWART

The Canadian Publishers
McClelland and Stewart Limited
25 Hollinger Road
Toronto M4B 3G2

CANADIAN CATALOGUING IN PUBLICATION DATA

Scott, F. R. (Francis Reginald), 1899-
   The collected poems of F.R. Scott

Includes index.
ISBN 0-7710-8014-X (bound)
ISBN 0-7710-8015-8 (pbk.)

I. Title.

PS8537.C62A17 1981   C811'.54   C81-094644-0
PR9199.3.S36A17 1981

Printed and bound in Canada

For Marian

and
In Memoriam
Arthur Smith, 1902-1980

CONTENTS

I
Indications

SPRING FLAME

Through the glowing dark
She came
Like to an arrowhead
Of flame.

One of no fear
By a wood
Spoke to the old fire
In her blood.

And the brimming trees
Knew the bond
Between themselves and those two
On the ground.

POEM TALKING TO POET

"Write me a poem," you said.
So I sat by the window, minding my business.

After a little you asked,
"Will it be modern and free?"

"I cannot tell you beforehand," I answered.
"I am not master here."

I watched the trees carve nightmares in the night,
Heard dusty winds borrow the sound of tears.

      (Then it came, and so it was,
      And Lo! There it was!)

"Here is your poem," I said.
"I do not think it will live long."

You sighed, then trembled on my fingertips,
Being yourself the writing on the page.

BELOW QUEBEC

On the wet sand's edge
Little murmuring waves
Trouble the dulse and sedge
That the tide leaves.

Along the north shore
Sleep the dark hills
And what their dreams are
A cool wind tells.

But no other stirring
Than waves and wind
Makes for the heart a song
At this day's end.

No stream-swirl nor ebb
Of sea round these cold coasts
Speaks of the pulse and throb
In our close breasts,

Nor tells you what pain
The night would work
If I were alone
Under this old cloak.

THE TRAPPISTS

I like to think that in his quiet cell,
While others spend undedicated lives
Amid the world's affairs, the lone monk strives
By day and night to break the accursed spell
Of things material. In him doth dwell
A mind detached and calm that scarce survives
In our forc'd living; and this age derives
Forgotten solace from his chapel-bell.

But chiefly would I praise those holy men
Who hold a nearer intercourse with God
Through mute attendance to monastic ways.
Alone, in silent hours, they hear again
The still, small voice that pierc'd the storm-spent cloud
And calmed the troubled seer in olden days.

SILENCE

A wind-gust
Curls in at the open window.
The curtain moves lightly, and is still.
My face grows cool an instant.
I inhale the scent of pine.

Then the coolness passes, the pine-scent vanishes.
Night wraps me again in her familiar calm.

SONNET

Once when you gave me a new book to read
That you had read and loved, and thought to find
Close to the inner fancies of my mind,
Knowing how well with yours they were agreed,
I took it wonderingly, and sought with speed
A firelit chamber, cunningly designed
For midnight musings, and there pulled the blind
On the night's dark sorrow, paying the wind no heed;
And drew thence unbelieved delights, until
Upon one page I found your pencil-score.
Then instantly the spell of the tale was gone
In a surge of the blood, and feeling the volume still
Warm from your nearness, your hand's benison,
I stared into the fire, and read no more.

HE WALKED IN A WORLD

He walked in a world where trees were lissom and round,
Flowers were lips, and every bush was a breast.
It seemed he lay on a woman who lay upon ground
And the furl of grass was hair that his hand pressed.

So men move and are moved to the tune of an hour,
So is the body bound to the fertile earth,
And out of the love of loving rises a power
To carve the stone of an age, give new worlds birth.

FOUR MOMENTS

I

Stand by the window, Tyltyl,
Stand still by the old chintz curtains.

Tell the littlest diamond
It has wonder in its eyes.

But leave me to blow smoke rings
In a dusty corner.

II

Lay your hand, lay it gently on my arm,
For there is no stillness lovelier
Than the deliberate, fond
Reticence of soft fingers on an arm.

III

The little hump of her body
Untidied the bed.

She heard a chair creak
And a shoe drop.

And after
The wind cooled her.

IV

Close,
So close your breath is warm.

While slowly the
Clock
Ticks

Little one,
Little lovely one.

PROUD CELLIST

Are there quiverings
Of flesh and blood
Like taut strings
And hollow wood

Stirring to fragile
Form, that lingers
Beneath my agile
Bow and fingers?

In no woman
Is love lent
So beautiful an
Instrument.

None so lovely
In her moving,
None so wholly
Lost in loving.

A low note dying, and
Not yet dead
Is a lover's hand
Uncomforted.

A low note dying, and
Sunk to rest
Is a lover's hand
Still, on a breast.

MOMENT

Lift up your head
Osier-tip,
Stand up now on your curled toes
Stretching leaves eagerly to sun and sky.
For today I bent you down sharply
And drew you over the hand
Of her who lay with me in your green shadows.
Wind never kissed wind
More softly
Nor shall ever mothwing
More lightly
Brush a white lily.

POEM

Let us stay a moment
On the grass.
Love, let us be silent
While winds pass.

Nature has her whispers.
If you wait
She will tune your heart to hers,
Soon or late.

Only be not mindful
Of desires,
Be as a wind-harp, still,
With taut wires.

DARK TOMB

*("When the Ming emperors died, many of their concubines
were buried alive with them.")*

It is hard to lie awake
While you sleep.

It is hard, on this stone,
In this dark tomb.

"Little lily,
Flower of night,
For you an Empire is kept waiting."

So you used to whisper
While ministers clicked.

Your arms were tawny rays about me,
Rays of the sun.
Now I wait.

Shall I move this arm?

FANTASY

Love, in a burst of joy,
Took a hop, skip and a jump,
And describing an utterly fantastic curve
Lit on a mountain peak.
There he strung his bow with a gossamer thread,
Fashioned an arrow of mistletoe,
Tipped it with a briar thorn,
Tufted it with a dandelion seed,
And shot it – whish!
UP . . . Up . . . up . . . up . . . .
It fell to earth
In a blind mathematical curve,
And pierced the loricated heart of a cheesemonger.
Clumsily, uncontrollably, and quite improperly,
He planted a heavy kiss on the neck of his youngest dairy-maid.
Whereat his wife, a maliciously observant woman,
Stunned him with a savoury Stilton.
So love unstrung his bow,
Recalled the errant shaft,
Broke the gossamer thread,
Replaced the briar thorn,
Planted the dandelion seed,
And sorrowfully removed to the Vale of Innocent Shadows.

XXX

Is a tree kinder than a doormat
With frayed edges?
Kinder than the worn corners
Trodden all to pieces?
Kinder than the black marks
Where the boots rubbed?

I have seen housemaids beating doormats:
Housemaids do not beat trees.
Neither do dogs sleep in trees,
But I have seen dogs sleeping on doormats,
Big dogs, puppy dogs, and warm black spaniels,
And when flies come
They snap at them.

Trees have only birds, and insects, and crawly things.
There is no humanity in these,
Only evolution, and sentimental poetry.
But in doormats there is much
Humanity
Vulgarity
Futility
Dust, boot-marks and sunlight.

ADIEUX À DEUX

The clock struck, showering the night's remonstrances
On his impoverished ears.
He felt the claws of his fears, and rose in a daze
From the warm wide impenetrable wound of her side,
And faced the town's bright maze, unpacified.

She said – Standing by the half-drawn blind
You are a half man against a box of stars.

The trivial phrase
Nudged an elbow in his mind,
Catching him unawares.
He knew the was from the is.
Something died in him that was hers
And something prevailed that was his.

Under her helpless gaze
He did not relent.
Yet he went out in a torment,
Crushing a dream on every step of the stairs.

BOURGEOIS BURIAL

The motor hearse nips in between
A street car and a traffic cop.
It leaves a smell of gasoline
And flaunts a crucifix on top.

Carry him off with a roar of gears.
He would choose no other hymn,
He who was set on the rim of things
With controls out of reach of his hand.
Fling him, a worn spare part, on the scrap-heap,
This he would understand.

But the crucifix? He will sleep
No better for this pious token.
This was no parcel of his life.
Now he is broken.

MIRANDA

Miranda's undiminished
By any sense of sin,
She does not circumscribe herself.
The thoughts her mind puts on

And all her pretty whimsies
Emancipated run,
She has no system but herself,
No ether but her own.

She's saner than September,
More single than the sky.
I do not think that someone
Could love her more than I.

I saw her on a Sunday
So maiden on a path
It was a peal of laughter
To understand her worth.

That night the thing that happened
Would set an aunt to stare:
We lay distinct as spinsters
Yet close as kisses are.

And on the Monday morning
By none but poplars seen
We hung our clothes on tree-tops.
Less maiden, but more mine,

We shared our joy in daylight
Beneath a leafy sun.
Perhaps there was a squirrel
Saw us – but he has gone.

THE CLEARING

Growing old is a withdrawing
    From the fire
In the little clearing
    Of desire.

It is moving to cooler
    Air on the fringe
Where trees are nearer
    And voices strange.

We need not shudder
    Or be afraid
Till we cross the border
    Of that dark wood.

Till in the dark glow
    Suddenly
We find the shadow
    Become the tree.

II
Laurentian

"We passed in silence, and the lake
We left without a name."
— F.G. Scott

NEW PATHS

Child of the North,
Yearn no more after old playthings,
Temples and towers and gates
Memory-haunted thoroughfares and rich palaces
And all the burdensome inheritance, the binding legacies,
Of the Old World and the East.

Here is a new soil and a sharp sun.

Turn from the past,
Walk with me among these indigent firs,
Climb these rough crags
And let winds that have swept lone cityless plains,
Gathering no sad tales of past endeavour,
Tell you of fresh beauty and full growth.

OLD SONG

far voices
and fretting leaves
this music the
hillside gives

but in the deep
Laurentian river
an elemental song
for ever

a quiet calling
of no mind
out of long aeons
when dust was blind
and ice hid sound

only a moving
with no note
granite lips
a stone throat

FROST IN AUTUMN

When the first ominous cold
Stills the sweet laughter of the northern lakes,
And the fall of a crisp leaf
Marks the eternal victory of death,
In the presence of granite mountains,
Ice-rounded valleys and rock shores,
I cannot bring myself to your embrace.

For love is an impudent defiance
Flung into the teeth of time,
A brazen denial
Of the omnipotence of death,
And here death whispers in the silences,
And a deep reverence is due to time.

SURFACES

This rock-bound river, ever flowing
Obedient to the ineluctable laws,
Brings a reminder from the barren north
Of the eternal lifeless processes.
There is an argument that will prevail
In this calm stretch of current, slowly drawn
Toward its final equilibrium.

Come, flaunt the brief prerogative of life,
Dip your small civilized foot in this cold water
And ripple, for a moment, the smooth surface of time.

NEW NAMES

Let us give new names
To the stars.
What does Venus mean
Or Mars?

The tall pines on the hill
Have seen no blood.
Beneath them no men or maids
Have woo'd.

Who would read old myths
By this lake
Where the wild duck paddle forth
At daybreak?

I am more moved by the lake sheen
When night is come
Than by all the tales of Babylon
Or Rome.

Look! The moon's path is broken
By rippling bars.
I think we should give new names
To the stars.

(1935)

LAURENTIAN

Timber pillow
Bed of stone
Sand the lake waves
Break upon

At my back
A smooth rock cover
This will do till
Night is over

Here no touch
Of limb or lip
Woman whisper
Dreamy sleep

Only a roving
Lover's hand
Over ribbed and
Sloping sand

Only the old cool lap
Of water
Dying to utter silence
After

Where dark fir trees
Thrusting high
To probe the mystery
Of sky

Are tall pinnacles
Erect
That speak familiar
Dialect

Night and thrusting
Dark tree meeting
These be tokens
Of my mating

AUTUMNAL

October is the month of dead leaves falling
Beautifully to lie upon grey rock and ground.
Death curves most carefully from the sky in this season
To lay a memory at the roots of trees.

Leaves curl and die, and dying
Give richly back their store of summer green
To strengthen parent stem, as lovers plant
Their seed for ancestry.
But love itself, life's greenest stratagem,
Though ever new, like leaves, is seasonal.

This we were told. Today we understand.

Why do you break a dry leaf in your hand?
Stand still awhile with me and hear
How from old hills the wind
Blows cold, bearing no sound
Of life striving in leaf,
Of root probing in ground,
Water calling, sap lifting.
October is dead and falling;
Soon snow will be drifting.

SNOWDRIFT

Set your proud mouth
Snowdrift!
Curve the knife-edge
Of your lip
To a thin, imperious smile.

The sun mounts high today.

NOVEMBER POOL

Sombre and very still
You have lain,
Frowning at the wind's will,
Angry at the rain.

Now winter frosts will bring
Cold ecstasies.
Well you know not even spring
Gives so wild a kiss.

NORTH STREAM

Ice mothers me
My bed is rock
Over sand I move silently.

I am crystal clear
To a sunbeam.
No grasses grow in me
My banks are clean.

Foam runs from the rapid
To rest on my dark pools.

TREES IN ICE

these gaunt prongs and points of trees
pierce the zero air with flame
every finger of black ice
stealing the sun's drawn fire
to make a burning of a barren bush

underneath
            from
                  still
flakes   branch
        of   and
            light   arm
fleck-   fall
      ing   fall
          the
            dark
                  white
                        snow

this cruelty is a formal loveliness
on a tree's torn limbs
this glittering pain

MARCH FIELD

Now the old folded snow
Shrinks from black earth.
Now is thrust forth
Heavy and still
The field's dark furrow.

Not yet the flowing
The mound-stirring
Not yet the inevitable flow.

There is a warm wind, stealing
From blunt brown hills, loosening
Sod and cold loam
Round rigid root and stem.

But no seed stirs
In this bare prison
Under the hollow sky.

The stone is not yet rolled away
Nor the body risen.

NORTH APRIL

The wind! Feel the wind!

Frozen snow-ridges
Under foot
Tunnelled ice-edges
Sounding hollow under foot

What is that in the wind!

Shadow-cool by sun-warmth
Glitter-light by sharp-shade
Bare tree limbs waving
Thrusting into the round sky
The blue vault fan-vaulted
With dark arches

The wind, what is that in the wind!

Snowbanks caving
Little delicate ice-films
Dropping, falling,
Dark pools of ice
In grey corners
Little streams running and flickering
In the sun

What is that! What is that!
There, in the wind!

Blue by white, blue in white,
White light, blue shadow,
Laughingly blue is the sky
White are the level fields
The piled mounds
The roadway is carved
With blue sky-pools

O the wind, the wind!
Tell me, flickering streams,
Tell me, dark ice-pools
Tell me, tree-arches, road-pools,
What is that in the wind!

A soul-stirring
A blood-coursing
The murmur of frost-free waters breaking
On far seashores
A baring of breasts long covered
A slipping of clothes from the dark earth-body
A coming of nakedness and love
Stark beauty soft-heralded
By warm winds

We come, we come, naked fields
We shall warm you, O dark earth-body
We shall clothe you with love
We shall cover you with the green fruit of our love.

ABSTRACT

Sharply place a cube edgewise
By a still, dark water.

Let the tall cone float on a disc of stone.

Peel bark from trees so broken stems can stare
At the winged skeleton of the extinct bird
Poised, angular, over the moon-bright rock.

GREY MORNING

The moan of wind over ground
The low round palpable sound of water
Rolling down upon stone, over and down,
And birches moving in the moving air
Came to me at dawn on that grey morning
Like an unutterable, primeval warning,
Like a burden too heavy to bear.

PARADISE LOST

Before any tree grew
On the ground,
Or clip of bird wing
Made sound,

Before cool fish drove
Under wave,
Or any cave-man
Made cave,

The clean aimless worlds
Spun true and blind
Unseen and undisturbed
By mind,

Till some expanding molecule
Of odd construction
Learned the original sin
Of reproduction,

Troubling the constant flow
With new activity,
Something beyond the grave
And more than gravity.

And so in shallow bays
And warm mud
Began the long tale
Of bone and blood.

The tale of man alive
And loth to die,
Of mine and thine and ours,
And the question, Why?

This was the turn of the tide,
The fall from heaven,
The spear in the side of God,
And time's division.

LAKESHORE

The lake is sharp along the shore
Trimming the bevelled edge of land
To level curves; the fretted sands
Go slanting down through liquid air
Till stones below shift here and there
Floating upon their broken sky
All netted by the prism wave
And rippled where the currents are.

I stare through windows at this cave
Where fish, like planes, slow-motioned, fly.
Poised in a still of gravity
The narrow minnow, flicking fin,
Hangs in a paler, ochre sun,
His doorways open everywhere.

And I am a tall frond that waves
Its head below its rooted feet
Seeking the light that draws it down
To forest floors beyond its reach
Vivid with gloom and eerie dreams.

The water's deepest colonnades
Contract the blood, and to this home
That stirs the dark amphibian
With me the naked swimmers come
Drawn to their prehistoric womb.

They too are liquid as they fall
Like tumbled water loosed above
Until they lie, diagonal,
Within the cool and sheltered grove
Stroked by the fingertips of love.

Silent, our sport is drowned in fact
Too virginal for speech or sound
And each is personal and laned
Along his private aqueduct.

50

Too soon the tether of the lungs
Is taut and straining, and we rise
Upon our undeveloped wings
Toward the prison of our ground
A secret anguish in our thighs
And mermaids in our memories.

This is our talent, to have grown
Upright in posture, false-erect,
A landed gentry, circumspect,
Tied to a horizontal soil
The floor and ceiling of the soul;
Striving, with cold and fishy care
To make an ocean of the air.

Sometimes, upon a crowded street,
I feel the sudden rain come down
And in the old, magnetic sound
I hear the opening of a gate
That loosens all the seven seas.
Watching the whole creation drown
I muse, alone, on Ararat.

see Can. L.P. No 87
(also article on Layton.)

PICNIC

Leaping from crowded car
We strip our calendar
Throw heavy years aside
And take a country stride.

The birds, our merriment,
Applaud with swift ascent,
Sing Gloria in curves
And Pegasus our hooves.

Our springing steps repeat
The flowers at our feet.
The youngest in our rout
Darts like a little trout.

No insect, worm or weed
Too hidden for our heed.
We stoop, and steal a look
In crevices of bark.

Our eyes are quick to tell
The acorn in its shell,
The pebble deep in pool,
The minnows all in school.

The trail soon joins a ledge
Upon a lake's cool edge,
Where, in the shade, we pick
A most pre-Cambrian nick.

Then is the granite spread
With ceremonial bread
And simple food we bless
With sauce of wilderness.

One with a priest's desire
To worship at a fire,
Rejecting with true scorn,
The shame of paper torn

Takes birchbark, balsam dead,
As tinder for his need,
With little twigs that bite
Upon a tiny light,

And by the ancient blaze
The warmth of ancient ways
Unwraps the urban cloth
That screens us from the earth.

The light and northern breeze
Has words to bring from trees,
And where the mountains run
The silent rhythm is sprung.

Far out, the water shines
In unrecorded lines,
That write upon the ground
With every patient sound.

The quiet of the land
Touches us with its hand.
As the failing sun goes down
Each one is left alone.

The happy children know
All this is theirs, for now.
Ours not all ours, who wear
The gloves of earlier.

STONE

A stone is a tomb
with the door barred.

A still picture
from a flick of motion.

A stone is a closed eye
reflecting what it saw.

Its smoothness
is an icy history.

A priest in a pulpit
and a solid sermon.

In the laboratory
a stone writes
its own epitaph.

A prison, is stone,
the inmates in chains.

When an atom of stone bursts
Hiroshima flames.

VAGRANT

he fled beyond the outer star
to spaces where no systems are

beyond the last accepted norm
the final vestiges of form

the compass of his mind   astute
to find a polar absolute
patrolled a mute circumference

the present seemed the only tense

there was no downwards for his feet
even his lust was obsolete

infinity became his own
himself the sole criterion

and he   the last dot in the sky
did but accentuate an i

now you may see him   virginal
content to live in montreal.

TRANS CANADA

Pulled from our ruts by the made-to-order gale
We sprang upward into a wider prairie
And dropped Regina below like a pile of bones. (original
name of
Regina)

Sky tumbled upon us in waterfalls,
But we were smarter than a Skeena salmon
And shot our silver body over the lip of air
To rest in a pool of space
On the top storey of our adventure.

A solar peace
And a six-way choice. 4 direction + up, down

Clouds, now, are the solid substance,
A floor of wool roughed by the wind
Standing in waves that halt in their fall.
A still of troughs.

The plane, our planet,
Travels on roads that are not seen or laid
But sound in instruments on pilots' ears,
While underneath
The sure wings
Are the everlasting arms of science.

Man, the lofty worm, tunnels his latest clay,
And bores his new career.

This frontier, too, is ours.
This everywhere whose life can only be led
At the pace of a rocket (destructive force, then)
Is common to man and man.
And every country below is an I land.

The sun sets on its top shelf,
And stars seem farther from our nearer grasp.

I have sat by night beside a cold lake
And touched things smoother than moonlight on still water,
But the moon on this cloud sea is not human,
And here is no shore, no intimacy,
Only the start of space, the road to suns.

(1943)

[handwritten annotation: human? maybe he's so into technology]

LANDING

Down
Far down through the clouds
Through their eye-holes
My land looked up at me
Beautiful, bare, clean, cold.

The top of the clouds
Was country too
A prairie in a clearer sun
But we must always leave the clouds
And land
On our land.

LAURENTIAN SHIELD

Hidden in wonder and snow, or sudden with summer,
This land stares at the sun in a huge silence
Endlessly repeating something we cannot hear.
Inarticulate, arctic,
Not written on by history, empty as paper,
It leans away from the world with songs in its lakes
Older than love, and lost in the miles.

This waiting is wanting.
It will choose its language
When it has chosen its technic,
A tongue to shape the vowels of its productivity.

A language of flesh and roses.

Now there are pre-words,
Cabin syllables,
Nouns of settlement
Slowly forming, with steel syntax,
The long sentence of its exploitation.

The first cry was the hunter, hungry for fur,
And the digger for gold, nomad, no-man, a particle;
Then the bold command of monopolies, big with machines,
Carving their kingdoms out of the public wealth;
And now the drone of the plane, scouting the ice,
Fills all the emptiness with neighbourhood
And links our future over the vanished pole.

But a deeper note is sounding, heard in the mines,
The scattered camps and the mills, a language of life,
And what will be written in the full culture of occupation
Will come, presently, tomorrow,
From millions whose hands can turn this rock into children.

MOUNT ROYAL

No things sit, set, hold. All swim,
Whether through space or cycle, rock or sea.
This mountain of Mount Royal marks the hours
On earth's sprung clock. Look how where
This once was island, lapped by salty waves,
And now seems fixed with sloping roads and homes.
Where flowers march, I dig these tiny shells
Once deep-down fishes safe, it seemed, on sand.
What! Sand, mud, silt, where now commuters go
About their civic clatter! Boulevards
Where crept the shiny mollusc! Time is big
With aeon seconds now, its pendulum
Swung back to ice-pressed pole-cap, that drove down
This chest of earth, until the melting came
And left a hollow cavity for seas
To make into a water waiting-room.
But sea-bed floated slowly, surely up
As weight released brought in-breath back to earth
And ground uprising drove the water back
In one more tick of clock. Pay taxes now,
Elect your boys, lay out your pleasant parks,
You gill-lunged, quarrelsome ephemera!
The tension tightens yearly, underneath,
A folding continent shifts silently
And oceans wait their turn for ice or streets.

ICEBERG

Dropped from its sloping womb
a huge cliff of blue
it roars its birth into an ocean
of slow death
returning
its giant pride
to deep water
recycling silently
its self-destructive art.

THE BIRD

Fluffed and still as snow, the white
bird lay in a crumple of death
far, far below the flock which, sailing, heard
but did not feel, the shot.

And the lonely boy suddenly grew afraid
as from his feet the doubt took wing and rose
up from the feathered hurt like a black bird
darkening the whole sky in the empty land.

WINTER SPARROWS

Feathered leaves
on a leafless bush.
Dropping to feed
they fly back to the stems.

AUTUMN LAKE

the calm of water   becalmed
   flowed into me   covered me
                   easing
            what was hurting
                   far down

            at mid-lake
            a cone of shadow
      from the hill behind
touched a cone of colour
      mirrored on the water
         from the far shore

         and I was drawn
            to that point
   where shadow and reflection
            (two fingers)
               touched
      one and one formed one
            and conflict ended

            so   calmed
      I glided downward
               melting
         into the wholeness
            into the still
               centre

III
Overture

"Philosophers merely explain the world;
what is needed is to change it."
— Karl Marx

SOCIAL NOTES I, 1932

PROLOGUE

"We see thee rise, O Canada,
The true North, strong and free,
(Tralala-lala, tralala-lala, etc....)"

I

NATURAL RESOURCES

Come and see the vast natural wealth of this mine.
In the short space of ten years
It has produced six American millionaires
And two thousand pauperized Canadian families.

II

THE NEW PHILANTHROPY

This employer, who pays $9 a week for a ten-hour day,
Is exceedingly concerned
Lest Mr. Bennett should adopt the dole,
And so ruin the morale of the workers.

III

SUMMER CAMP

Here is a lovely little camp
Built among Canadian hills
By a Children's Welfare Society
Which is entirely supported by voluntary contributions.
All summer long underprivileged children scamper about.
And it is astonishing how quickly they look healthy and well.
Two weeks here in the sun and air
Through the kindness of our charity subscribers
Will be a wonderful help to the little tots
When they return for a winter in the slums.

IV
XMAS SHOPPING

It is so nice for people to give things at Christmas
That the stores stay open every evening till ten,
And the shop-girls celebrate the coming of Christ
By standing on their feet fourteen hours a day.

V
MODERN MEDICINE

Here is a marvellous new serum:
Six injections and your pneumonia is cured.
But at present a drug firm holds the monopoly
So you must pay $14 a shot – or die.

VI
JUSTICE

This judge is busy sentencing criminals
Of whose upbringing and environment he is totally ignorant.
His qualifications, however, are the highest –
A college course in Arts,
A technical training in law,
Ten years practice at the Bar,
And membership in the proper political party.
Who should know better than he
Just how many years in prison
Are needed to reform a slum-product,
Or how many strokes of the lash
Will put an end to assaults on young girls?

VII
LAND OF OPPORTUNITY

This young Polish peasant,
Enticed to Canada by a CPR advertisement
Of a glorified western homestead,
Spent the best years of his life

And every cent of his savings
Trying to make a living from Canadian soil.
Finally broken by the slump in wheat
He drifted to the city, spent six months in a lousy refuge,
Got involved in a Communist demonstration,
And is now being deported by the Canadian government.
This will teach these foreign reds
The sort of country they've come to.

VIII

TREASURE IN HEAVEN

Many ecclesiastics and pious persons
Draw dividends from this Power Corporation
Which underpays its workers and overcharges its consumers.
Nevertheless the sayings of the Master are obeyed,
For verily there is no rust on a Public Utility privately owned,
And the moth doth not corrupt its Class A Preferred Stock.

EPILOGUE*

*"I believe in Canada.
I love her as my home.
I honour her institutions.
I rejoice in the abundance of her resources....*

*To her products I pledge my patronage,
And to the cause of her producers
I pledge my devotion."*

(*From *My Creed*, issued by the Hon. H.H. Stevens, Minister of Trade
and Commerce, New Year's 1931.)

ODE TO A POLITICIAN

Item: A STURDY BOY

In simple cottage, with scant ceremonial,
Observe the birthday of this young colonial.

Clutching the nearest good as best he can
The helpless mite perceives no social plan.

He grows unhampered in his natural skills
And finds companionship in lakes and hills.

Item: A FORKED ROAD

But soon this native freedom meets its end
And his fresh mind to ancient rules must bend.

At school he learns the three Canadian things:
Obedience, Loyalty, and Love of Kings.

To serve a country other than his own
Becomes for him the highest duty known,

To keep antiquity alive forever
The proper object of his young endeavour.

Item: A YOUNG MAN'S COUNTRY

Hence though the Northland calls him to be free
He never sheds this first servility.

His keen ambition, after several knocks,
Soon finds an outlet in the orthodox.

He does not recognize the new frontiers
Which beckon, as of old, for pioneers.

So he is proud, not seeing the distant star,
To hitch his wagon to the CPR.

Item: DOING WELL

No matter if his income starts from scratch:
In this career he quickly strikes a match.

Proceeding on two rails that never meet
He lands eventually on easy street.

For not a miner digs or farmer sows
Unless to this steel fist some tribute flows.

Item: DOING GOOD

Now full success has brought him wealth and ease
With lots of honorary LL.D.'s.

From this advantage point, still hale and hearty,
He ties his fortune to the Tory Party.

And in return for this attractive feeder
The party promptly chooses him as leader.

The public follow at the next election;
So there he reigns – the national selection.

Item: MORE BUSINESS IN GOVERNMENT

Canadians now have picked to run their state
The sort of man who "made their country great."

Once in the saddle, swift the whip he cracks.
The Mounties spring like thistles in his tracks.

When fools complain, or some poor victims squeal,
He meets their protest with an iron heel.

A simple rule for markets he discovers:
To close his own and blast his way to others.

To keep our credit good and money sound
Some novel democratic ways are found.

The rich are paid by taxes on the poor;
The unemployed are chased from door to door;

The wages fall though dividends are earned,
And people starve though surplus food is burned.

Item: A FLICKER OF DOUBT

This chaos kept alive by penal laws
In time gives even our politician pause.

Some glimmering concept of a juster state
Begins to trouble him – but just too late.

His whole life work had dug the grave too deep
In which the people's hopes and fortunes sleep.

Item: AN EPITAPH

To make the single meaning doubly clear
He ends the journey – as a British peer.

SOCIAL NOTES II, 1935

I
EFFICIENCY

The efficiency of the capitalist system
Is rightly admired by important people.
Our huge steel mills
Operating at 25 per cent of capacity
Are the last word in organization.
The new grain elevators
Stored with superfluous wheat
Can unload a grain-boat in two hours.
Marvellous card-sorting machines
Make it easy to keep track of the unemployed.
There isn't one unnecessary employee
In these textile plants
That require a 75 per cent tariff protection.
And when our closed shoe factories re-open
They will produce more footwear than we can possibly buy.
So don't let's start experimenting with socialism
Which everyone knows means inefficiency and waste.

II
MOTHERHOOD

Her travail now over
And her brood gone far away
This old woman of fifty
Must go charring at $2 a day.

III
EXPERT ADVICE

Have you ever noticed
How many members of religious orders
Who have taken perpetual vows
Of poverty
And chastity
Now spend their time defending private property
And urging the poor to have large families?

IV
COMING HOME

The Soviet ship from Leningrad to London
Was called the Co-operation,
But to reach democratic Canada
I travelled by the Duchess of Richmond.

V
GREAT DISCOVERY

After ten years of research
This great scientist
Made so valuable a discovery
That a big corporation actually paid him $150,000
To keep it off the market.

VI
OBSERVATION

In tonight's newspaper
There were two protests:
One by an Archbishop
Against the spread of communism,
And one by an unemployed man
Who said his children were sleeping four in a bed
To keep warm.

VII
GOVERNMENT HELP

After the strike began
Troops were rushed
To defend property.
But before the trouble started
Nobody seems to have bothered
To defend living standards.

VIII

GENERAL ELECTION

There is nothing like hard times
For teaching the people to think.
By a decisive vote
After discussing all the issues
They have turned out the Conservatives
And put back the Liberals.

HANGED BY THE NECK

When a man is to be hanged
The professionals order themselves
In ritual rank.
Above, with the victim,
Stand the Law and the Church
To assist at the killing,
While under the scaffold
The Doctor waits
To receive his trussed patient
And to test
Without healing
The pace of his lingering death.

THE BARONS

The Barons
    Make
Applause they
    Take,

And pay for
    Peals
That hide their
    Steals.

They buy the
    Press
In which they
    Stress

The press must
    Be
Unbought and
    Free.

This is their
    Test
Of what is
    Best –

Whatever
    Fills
Their vaults and
    Tills.

They push their
    Rule
To church and
    School,

Are they not
        Guardians,
Trustees and
        Wardens?

Their bread-lines
        Take
The men they
        Break,

Their prisons
        Seal
The fools who
        Squeal.

Their needs
        Dictate
Affairs of
        State,

Their lobbies
        Bend
The forward
        Trend,

And laws'
        Command
Protects their
        Hand.

While we with
        Arms
Defend their
        Homes,

Their fingers
        Force
The public
        Purse.

Though parties
        Strain,
The barons
        Reign.

Though planners
        Plan
The barons
        Ban.

For them, the
        Swag;
For us, the
        Bag.

For them, the
        Loot;
For us, the
        Boot.

DISINHERITED

These that tried to lead us and failed,
These holders of office out of the past
Let them join the past.

Not to recognize when the past is past
Is our concentration camp.

Let us refuse the estate
Opened by the death of an era,
Cluttered with debts, privileges,
And mammoth corporations labelled "free enterprise."

Let us cut ourselves off with the shilling of equality.
And take as our portion a people's broadacre.

TO CERTAIN FRIENDS

I see my friends now standing about me, bemused,
Eyeing me dubiously as I pursue my course,
Clutching their little less that is worlds away.

Full of good will, they greet me with offers of help,
Now and then with the five-dollar bill of evasion,
Sincere in their insincerity; believing in unbelief.

The nation's needs are to them considerable problems.
Often they play no bridge nor sit at the movies,
Preferring to hear some expert discuss every angle.

They show great zeal collecting the news and statistics.
They know far more about every question than I do,
But their knowledge of how to use knowledge grows smaller and
    smaller.

They make a virtue of having an open mind,
Open to endless arrivals of other men's suggestions,
To the rain of facts that deepens the drought of the will.

Above all they fear the positive formation of opinion,
The essential choice that acts as a mental compass,
The clear perception of the road to the receding horizon.

For this would mean leaving the shade of the middle ground
To walk in the open air, and in unknown places;
Might lead, perhaps – dread thought! – to definite action.

They will grow old seeking to avoid conclusions,
Refusing to learn by living, to test by trying,
Letting opportunities slip from their tentative fingers,

Till one day, after the world has tired of waiting,
While they are busy arguing about the obvious,
A half-witted demagogue will walk away with their children.

W.L.M.K.

How shall we speak of Canada,
Mackenzie King dead?
The Mother's boy in the lonely room
With his dog, his medium and his ruins?

He blunted us.

We had no shape
Because he never took sides,
And no sides
Because he never allowed them to take shape.

He skilfully avoided what was wrong
Without saying what was right,
And never let his on the one hand
Know what his on the other hand was doing.

The height of his ambition
Was to pile a Parliamentary Committee on a Royal Commission,
To have "conscription if necessary
But not necessarily conscription,"
To let Parliament decide –
Later.

Postpone, postpone, abstain.

Only one thread was certain:
After World War I
Business as usual,
After World War II
Orderly decontrol.
Always he led us back to where we were before.

He seemed to be in the centre
Because we had no centre,
No vision
To pierce the smoke-screen of his politics.

Truly he will be remembered
Wherever men honour ingenuity,
Ambiguity, inactivity, and political longevity.

Let us raise up a temple
To the cult of mediocrity,
Do nothing by halves
Which can be done by quarters.

GENERAL ELECTION 1958

Do you suffer from arthritic pain, collapse of prices, atomic fall-out?
The Tories will bring you fast, Fast, FAST relief.
The Tories have not one analgesic but three analgesics –
High tariffs for low incomes, low taxes for high incomes,
And a flow of natural gas piped from Prince Albert.
So switch off Uncle Louis and tune in Honest John,
See the new vision, change the name of your brand,
Go to the drugstore today, follow the crowd,
Take home the handy pack or family carton.
When the Grey Cup is over the Stanley Cup begins
And next year the Queen Mother will visit the unemployed.

"Emergency, emergency," I cried, "give us emergency,
This shall be the doctrine of our salvation.
Are we not surrounded by emergencies?
The rent of a house, the cost of food, pensions and health, the
    unemployed,
These are lasting emergencies, tragic for me."
But the only answer was "Property and Civil Rights,"
And all my peace-time troubles were counted as nothing.
"At least you have an unoccupied field," I urged,
"Or something ancillary for a man with four children?
Surely my insecurity and want affect the body politic?"
But back came the echo of "Property and Civil Rights."
I was told to wrap my sorrows in watertight compartments.
"Please, please," I entreated, "look at my problem.
I and my brothers, regardless of race, are afflicted.
Our welfare hangs on remote policies, distant decisions,
Planning of trade, guaranteed prices, high employment;
Can provincial fractions govern this complex whole?
Surely such questions are now supra-national!"
But the judges fidgeted over their digests
And blew me away with the canons of construction.
"This is intolerable," I shouted, "this is one country;
Two flourishing cultures, but joined in one nation.
I demand peace, order and good government,
This you must admit is the aim of Confederation!"
But firmly and sternly I was pushed to a corner
And covered with the wet blanket of provincial autonomy.
Stifling under the burden I raised my hands to heaven
And called out with my last and expiring breath
"At least you cannot deny I have a new aspect?
I cite in my aid the new approach of Lord Simon!"
But all I could hear was the old sing-song,
This time in Latin, muttering *stare decisis*.

PRIZES

Prizes are gifts from the old
To the young who are old.

Those who have arrived
Search in the mirror of youth
For their own reflection.
Bravo! Bravo!

But oh there is a prize, a crown, for some
That stems of wood, and bears the sharpest thorn.

CHARITY

A code of laws
Lies written
On this beggar's hand.

My small coin
Lengthens
The harsh sentence.

I AM EMPLOYED

by my idea of myself. I conceive
work in an office, so I arrive,
hang my coat on a peg, ring for a girl.
She too is but a thought of herself, though she comes in the flesh,
and poses a little as she hands me the mail.
I have a plan of the day's activities –
A to meet, B to write, C to avoid. I obey.

Where is the first button that starts the wheels?
Though all is available, nothing is taken
that is not pre-selected, hence the insubstantial
is the practical, the theory all-important,
and the routines, subconscious theories,
wall up the doorways slowly, one by one.

How hard to strike against this management,
picket one's habits, unionize dreams,
down tools and march into the thoroughfares
holding the banner high: UNFAIR TO MYSELF.

ARCHIVE

Table this document: to wit, one page
Found in the odd detritus of this age.
A simple chapter, in the English tongue,
Of normal length and paragraphed. Begun
In gentle language, probing for the heart,
But soon involuntarily made a part
Of social change and crisis; men at war
Defending systems rotten at the core.
Everywhere in the world the battle waged
Before the deeper issues had been gauged.

The personal pronoun does not count in this tale.
Before so great upheavals love grows pale,
The precious ego shivers in the storm.
Footnotes for sociologists are here,
And writing FINIS I shall drop no tear
Though I am the name, the content, and the form.

MURAL

When shepherds cease to watch their flocks
And tend instead bacterial stocks;
When farmers learn in chemic schools
To architect the molecules;
When all our food comes fresh and clean
From some unbreakable machine,
And crops are raised in metal trays
Beneath the ultra-violet rays;
When eggs are laid in numbered tens
Without the cluck of boasting hens,
And from the cool assembly-lines
Come wormless fruits and vintaged wines;
When honey drips in plastic cone
With none but a mechanic drone,
And vitamins by legal right
Are bedded in each measured bite;
When cloths are spun from glass and trees
And girls are clad with engine ease,
And men in rockets leave the ground
To fly the pole with single bound;
When ova swell in Huxleyan tubes,
Paternal sperm is sold in cubes,
And babies nuzzle buna taps
As sucklings now the unsterile paps;
When rules of health need not espouse
The ventral processes of cows,
And man is parasite no more
On some less clever herbivore;
When sheep and cattle graze at will
As decorations on the hill,
And all the natural creatures roam
As pets within their zoo-like home;
When by some microscopic means
Genetecists control the genes
And coloured skin and crinkly hair
Are choices for each bridal pair —
Then, on the Eden air, shall come

A gentle, low, electric hum,
Apotheosis of the Wheel
That cannot think and cannot feel,
A lingering echo of the strife
That crushed the old pre-technic life.
Then poverty shall be a word
Philologists alone have heard,
The slightest want shall know its fill,
Desire shall culminate in skill.
The carefree lovers shall repair
To halls of air-conditioned air
And tune-in coloured symphonies
To prick their elongated bliss.
Man shall arise from dialled feast
Without the slaughter of a beast;
His conscience smooth as metal plate
Shall magnify his stainless state;
His bloodless background shall be blest
With a prolonged, inventive rest.
All violence streamlined into zeal
For one colossal commonweal.

PRESS REPORT

Are these my words, recorded
      So incomplete?
Is all my thought rewarded
      With such deceit?

Great issues in this season
      Compel a choice,
And to the search for reason
      I add my voice.

But with a twist of headline
      The lie is said,
And truth upon the deadline
      Lies wholly dead.

ECLIPSES

We watched the sun behind the moon
And tested theories in the dark.
The slightest change in the event
Improved the estimated mark.

Beside us frocked and righteous men
Proclaimed their absolutes as laws.
They kept their purity of creed
By twisting facts that showed the flaws.

OVERTURE

In the dark room, under a cone of light,
You precisely play the Mozart sonata. The bright
Clear notes fly like sparks through the air
And trace a flickering pattern of music there.

Your hands dart in the light, your fingers flow.
They are ten careful operatives in a row
That pick their packets of sound from steel bars
Constructing harmonies as sharp as stars.

But how shall I hear old music? This is an hour
Of new beginnings, concepts warring for power,
Decay of systems – the tissue of art is torn
With overtures of an era being born.

And this perfection which is less yourself
Than Mozart, seems a trinket on a shelf,
A pretty octave played before a window
Beyond whose curtain grows a world crescendo.

DEDICATION

From those condemned to labour
For profit of another
We take our new endeavour.

For sect and class and pattern
Through whom the strata harden
We sharpen now the weapon.

Till power is brought to pooling
And outcasts share in ruling
There will not be an ending
Nor any peace for spending.

CREED

The world is my country
The human race is my race
The spirit of man is my God
The future of man is my heaven

IV
Conflict

"The aftermath is our joint child."

TORPEDO DESCENDING

Past the frail steel goal
Of its grim intent
This torpedo
Swims, remote and spent,

A touchy volcano,
Thin and sinister,
Loosed by the proud talk
Of some cabinet minister.

Engineers lucubrated,
Mechanics sweated,
Rulers waxed righteous,
Cruisers pirouetted,

That this arbiter
Of human squabbles
Might become a fizzle
Of expiring bubbles.

Shed no saline tear
Over its green vertical highway.
It will find a new world
Of kindlier clay.

WAR

Come never to the throes of this despair
Where men as infants break their dearest toys,
Let not your mind its frontier search forswear
To plan sharp death for blind obedient boys.
Leave half-believers to affront the air
With deadly missile and the deadlier lies.
If war must come, let not your hand prepare
The ordered slaughter for the hollow prize.

Seek out the new; reform the stubborn past;
Select and build; discard the emblazoned shell.
Expand the narrow concept; shape the last;
Men's boasts belittle and their dreams compel.
Our warfare's not against, but for mankind;
Our falling ramparts, barriers of the mind.

LEST WE FORGET

The British troops at the Dardanelles
Were blown to bits by British shells
    Sold to the Turks by Vickers.
And many a brave Canadian youth
Will shed his blood on foreign shores,
And die for Democracy, Freedom, Truth,
With his body full of Canadian ores,
Canadian nickel, lead, and scrap,
Sold to the German, sold to the Jap,
    With Capital watching the tickers.

For these we too are bleeding: the homes burning,
The schools broken and ended, the vision thwarted,
The youths, their backs to the wall, awaiting the volley,
The child staring at a huddled form.

And Guernica, more real than our daily bread.

For these our hurt and hate, sharp couriers,
Arouse a waking world: the black crusade,
Pious brutality, mass massacre,
Sudden cohesion of class, wealth and creed,
Behind the gilded cross, the swastika,
Behind neutrality, the will to kill.

And Lorca, rising godlike from fascist guns.

In the spring of ideas they were, the rare spring
That breaks historic winters. Street and field
Stirring with hope and green with new endeavour,
The cracking husks copious with sprouting seed.
Here was destruction before flowering,
Here freedom was cut in its first tendrils.

This issue is not ended with defeat.

CONFLICT

When I see the falling bombs
Then I see defended homes.
Men above and men below
Die to save the good they know.

Through the wrong the bullets prove
Shows the bravery of love.
Pro and con have single stem
Half a truth dividing them.

Between the dagger and the breast
The bond is stronger than the beast.
Prison, ghetto, flag and gun
Mark the craving for the One.

Persecution's cruel mouth
Shows a twisted love of truth.
Deeper than the rack and rope
Lies the double human hope.

My good, your good, good we seek
Though we turn no other cheek.
He who slays and he who's slain
Like in purpose, like in pain.

Who shall bend to single plan
The narrow sacrifice of man?
Find the vision and the urge
To make a thousand roads converge?

BOSTON TEA PARTY 1940

Beneath the hum of trivial talk
A rebel memory vainly stirs.
The hardened arteries of speech
Obstruct the paths the mind prefers.

The formalisms, cut as glass,
Sway gently on their silken thread
Emitting tinkles as we pass.
The embattled farmers long are dead.

The Harvard pundit's tea is brought
Amid the ample female forms.
He quits his crevices of thought
To taste the soft and simpler norms,

While D.A.R.'s and Ph.D's
And "How-d'ye-do's" and "Is-that-so's"
Are wafted on a scented breeze
That piles the orchid on the rose.

The English butler scarce is heard
Purveying the historic drink.
His servile mien, without a word,
Provides the true historic link

With colony and ruling class,
Commons by royalty dissolved,
Declared dependence of the mass
And revolution unrevolved.

O serve me, Butler, mild and meek,
Your gentle tea so piping hot.
No rebel here shall dare to speak,
And round this world, who hears a shot?

FLUX

Under the constant impact, the swift response.
We leap from crumbling footholds, gulfs below,
Or like the Arctic male seeking a pole
Traverse the sea-lanes when the floes touch.
Trained to the tram-line and the office walk,
The weekend outing and the game of bridge,
Little avails us now the trim routine.

Refugees of the mind load their loved bric-à-brac
Class gewgaws and their little tea-set faiths
On the piled ox-cart of tradition; make for the rear.
This self-imprisonment obstructs the roads
And only the mobile heart allows escape.

Now from each corner of their settled ways
Egos draw to the mass, millions move.
Robot men swarm in their steel shells
Over the crust of seven continents.
There's naught for me and you, only for us.

Strip for this venture forth, my pretty man.
Props and property are caving in.
The roar of masonry and smothered towns,
Ice-cap solitudes on money-marts
And four winds out of untested skies –
This is the thunder of the still small voice.

And if the ultimate I, the inner mind,
The only shelter proof against attack,
Sustain these days, carry this banner out
To the clumsy dawn: a green seed
Lies on the ground, under a leafless tree.

SPRING 1941

Dawn parts the womb of night. The sturdy sun
Is born leaping. Lucky dad, earth!
These are new days for men and worlds
And thought cuts highways into hinterlands.

Light rays fall right, are blunt. Now we can stride
Out in the clear. No palsy now,
No crutch or stick when banners are streaming.
The quicker pulse is quickness in the pace.
Must savour novelties, embrace unknowns,
These stellar flights make mites of old ideas.
Least move must rise to stratosphere. Down's up,
Hill is hole, underworld is tops.
Claims outnumber prizes, that is clear,
And castaways are soil for stronger seed.

Nip off fresh flowers quickly – they're away.
No stopping now in this foreblast.
With furrows deeper than the deepest root
This year we only crop millennials.

Take heart from thrust and throb, sown bed, clean leaf,
Green shoots that finger out from iron shells,
The dead pods' tiny thunder of despair
And spring's untouched intention, winter-free.

Give thanks for so much shedding down of death.
This pain's not penalty, but premature.
Blisters are burst now on all sorry places,
Pus runs fearful, fretful – let it run,
Sun's heat will sterilize the streptococks.
All of one piece this rush to kill and live.

Now spring flood covers old sticks,
Floats grounded tubs, breaks dams,
Sunders the dyke, opens the lock and dock,
Carries the surface boundaries to sea.

Much dirt is shifted over meadowland,
Much beauty buried down in muck and murk.
Too bad, no doubt, but never wait nor quit.
On's the way out, no other. On is free.
Drop token loads, but save the harder man,
Eyes to stare at the sun, heart's leap and love.
Nothing retards our march when fences go,
It's fast forward and over the hills to sky.
Are we born, too? Can we be born
Like sun from night, a fructifying fire?
Turn dark to fecundation, there is power!
And roll, roll over the springing world.

ARMAGEDDON

I

THE SHOCK

Suddenly the last boundary broke
And every land was used by somebody else.
The closed world swarmed with a throng of roads
Where caterpillars span a thread of our blood
And sewed our flags into the history-quilt.
The net of tracks tangled the volunteers
So every man fastened his cuffs of steel.
The clearest call came from the citadels,
Over the churches flew the black birds,
Trumpets blew but only echoes answered
And pamphlet thought scuttled from iron heels.
A lease of fight was lent to far friends,
Prodigious ways were found through sand and ice,
Boats rolled on land while engines swam
And dropping men captured the centre first.
Bound in their box of hate, all were packed
In neat grades, carded and grooved. The shape
Of mind and hand fitted the single die.
Less than a horde was nothing. Zeros grew
On integers, adding an ache of size.
Off assembly lines came motor-men
Held by rivets of fear. Identical cogs
Meshed in reverse directions, gathering speed,
Knotting distance into a lace for boots
That never trod upon ground.
A single shaft could use this force, one core
For such power would magnetize a world.
But segment thought died in the private zones,
Men read their fate upon their ancient dials
And neither the pain nor vision found its goal.

II
THE INSIGHT

This foe we fight is half of our own self.
He aims our gunsight as we shoot him down,
Sings our self-righteous hymns, is our own pride,
And writes our sentence in the green baize treaty.
See our metal cannon hang in the air
Over an Asian archipelago,
Dropping the tooled death on the enemy dot
Precisely, ending a threat, and are headlined home
Till the cheers penetrate
An industrial slum.
See the façade fall
From the recent ally under the show of force,
Quislings dancing on their reddening tape,
While underneath, in the clean despair,
The scribbled slogan burns on the public wall.

This line of cleavage runs across the fronts,
Turns back on the victor foe, doubles our task and hope,
Pierces our hearts, and in the secret thought
We deal the final blows. Out of this battle
Comes our resistance, out of this private invasion
Repelled, comes the demos flow of power.

III
THE PEOPLE'S WILL

It is white hot with our bright hurt, this torrent,
Molten will fitting our chosen mould
Shaped with the common hand in the common clay.
This is our conquest now, our enterprise.
No foreman foreign to our code or class
Takes this decision out of our union law.
We choose our leaders and select our foes
And nearest friend must pass our scrutiny.
We frame the path with the power, alter the shape

Of the overhead state to suit our solid claim.
If armies march, they are ours, if captains call
Over the Afric sands, they are our commands,
And the shouted cry heard in the jungle is ours.

We have changed this agony from our undoing
To our oncoming, the coil before the spring.

ENEMIES

Because we hate you
We cannot escape you,
We struggle to reach you.
Absorbed by your movements,
We study your plans,
We report every word you say.
Though determined to kill you
In destroying you we mate with you.
The aftermath is our joint child.

RECOVERY

Now thought seeks shelter, lest the heart melt
In the iron rain, the brain bend
Under the bombs of news.
Fearfully the mind's hands dig
In the débris of thought, for the lovely body of faith.
Is she alive after this shock, does she yet breathe?

O say that she lives, she is ours, imperishable,
Say that the crypt stood.

We had no right to hope, no claim to defence.
We had played in the hanging gardens, lain in the sun
On a roof of glass. We had given no thought
To the deep soil of the base, the sunken shafts
Resting on rock. We loved the façade
More than the wall, the ivy more than the stone.
We took our gifts for our gains; we fed without ploughing.

But she lives, it is true, the eyes glow.
The lips are firm under the pain, they move,
It is our name that is spoken.

O clutch her to you, bring her triumphant forth.
Stand by her side now, scatter the panzer doubts.
She is more dear after this swift assault,
More one and alone, an ultimate.
In her sure presence only is there strength.

This sharp blow pulls the excesses down,
Strips off the ornament, tightens the nerve,
Bares limbs for movement and the forward march.
More roads are opened than are closed by bombs
And truth stands naked under the flashing charge.

VILLANELLE FOR OUR TIME

From bitter searching of the heart,
Quickened with passion and with pain
We rise to play a greater part.

This is the faith from which we start:
Men shall know commonwealth again
From bitter searching of the heart.

We loved the easy and the smart,
But now, with keener hand and brain,
We rise to play a greater part.

The lesser loyalties depart,
And neither race nor creed remain
From bitter searching of the heart.

Not steering by the venal chart
That tricked the mass for private gain,
We rise to play a greater part.

Reshaping narrow law and art
Whose symbols are the millions slain,
From bitter searching of the heart
We rise to play a greater part.

FOR R.A.S. 1925-1943

He left the country that he loved so well,
Shawbridge, Piedmont, and the Tremblant runs,
And climbed to the centre of war by his own trail.
Barred from the easy virtue of enlistment
He fought a private battle for his chance to share the world's crisis.

On his way to the scenes of death, he met death.
Death reached out with an eagerness that matched his own.
Death violent, Atlantic, submarine.
The challenge so absolute was met absolutely.

It was as though there were special need to attend
To this boy's daring, as though if his will survived
We should survive too easily, win with too sudden success,
Win without understanding the fulness of our penalty.

He bore in his single hand the essence of our tragedy.

I tell you no one anywhere brought more than this.
Not the comrades who crouched shoulder to shoulder at Stalingrad,
Not Buerling, superb in his skill,
Nor the heroisms noted on the field of battle.

I write of him because he wished to write,
And because he had time only to pour
The table of his contents upon the historic water.

WAR NEWS

On every front, and in the reversing air
The guns and planes carry out argument.
None can resist. This is our feat of war.
This is our self-assertion. We are content.
We dress our purpose in the accustomed cloth
Whole cut from great abstractions, oversize.
We are immensely conscious of our worth
And ask no more than slaughtered enemies.
This is our one supreme desire, to find
The unconditionally-surrendered foe
Begging for mercy at our conquering heels.
Meanwhile the little wheels within the wheels
Mesh in the former grooves, the Churchills bow,
And weathering the gale, we foster the whirlwind.

FOR ALL THOSE DEAD

For all those dead who have no monument
Save their potentiality
I sing.
They have gone down while struggling to survive
And walked like ghosts upon their unmarked graves.

ORDERLY DECONTROL 1947

Above all, we must have "orderly decontrol."
No foolish rush and scramble to renounce
The prime functions of government. We must show
How carefully and consciously we can steer toward disaster,
Letting the forces of anarchy return one by one
    Through orderly decontrol.

First we must give away all the assets of war:
Stores, trucks, equipment, goods of every kind,
And all the factories built with public money.
These must be channelled toward monopolies,
Which will most surely exploit them. This we shall call
    Restoring free enterprise.

Then we must care for the housing needs of our people,
The Family being so sacred. What we need here
Is the freeing of private contractors, high interest rates
For insurance and mortgage companies. Thus we achieve
Incentives to build the luxury homes and apartments
    Fit for heroes to look at.

Since we are founding a more democratic society
We must raise the low incomes, anchor the cost of living.
So we withdraw all subsidies. Milk is now orderly.
Wages we leave to nine provinces. Labour must learn
Not to cut into profits. Thus we shall win
    The war on inflation.

We are most deeply concerned with national unity.
This is one country; the state has new obligations.
So we submit our national responsibilities
To the veto of provincial politicians. We shall worship
At the altar of divided jurisdiction, and thus we shall honour
    The Compact of Confederation.

LESSON

This is our gardening
And this our hardening:
There is no pardoning.

We shall not be forgiven
Because we have not striven.

This is our sowing
And this our knowing:
There is no growing.

There shall be great slaughtering
Because there was no watering.

He gave into our hand
New seed for every land:
We did not understand.

These innocents Thou starvest,
O Lord, Thou soon shalt harvest.

NO CURTAIN

From stone to arrow, sling-shot, gun,
Rifle and rocket, roadways run.
Hammer and sickle, old as fable,
Die with the smithy and the stable.

Creators of the live machine
We quit the lanes of what has been,
Forced by the atom and the jet
To cross the gulfs our hatreds set.

Laws are less quick
Than wheel and rod
To change the attributes
Of God.
This truth is certain:
Iron makes no curtain.

STREET CRY

Mushrooms!
Mushrooms!
Who'll buy
My mushrooms?
Fresh from
Los Alamos!
Very big,
One is enough,
Who'll buy?
Who'll buy?

DEGENERATION

The first to go are the niceties,
The little minor conformities
That suddenly seem absurdities.

Soon kindling animosities
Surmount the old civilities
And start the first brutalities.

Then come the bold extremities,
The justified enormities,
The unrestrained ferocities.

V
Journeys

ON THE DEATH OF GANDHI

India, India, I dreamed of your texture,
When a bullet, large as an army, tore through your heart.
The chord that broke loosened the holy rivers
And all the teeming lands were flooded with tears.

Your great one
Was close as though I could see and receive him.
Far away among my Canadian snows
The white of my landscape was tinged with his colour,
My mountains were taller.

I saw his road point to the goal of our freedom,
And I knew that we must aim
At the centre of his terrible simplicity
Or be condemned in our darkness to cower
Behind the walls of our little religions,
Shrinking from the shadow of our own untouchables.

This is my salute
To the towering truth of his vision:
Though evil had power to draw off his praying blood,
The doors of his temple have opened on all the world.

India, India, the load of your history
Presses down upon the springs of your progress,
For man is heir of his past, yet his spirit
Leaps, in an instant, over the Himalayas.

I read poems taken from old Indian tongues –
Bengali, Hindi, Telugu, Urdu, Kannada –
"Engraved with lines of agony"
Or with the "irrepressible desire to utter Omkar,"
The name of God,
And it seemed of me they were speaking.
When their tears fell, they poured out my anguish,
Far glories were mine on the Punjabi hills,
In the eyes of their women I saw the passion too.

Strange images were used. I do not know
"The thin branches of siris, amlaki, bocul and neem,"
Nor how "A baby vulture cries out in a banyan,"

But the image of the image is the same.
Where I sit now, against this Canadian sky,
Branches of maple and of elm are thin,
A cry goes up in the night,
And over in Caughnawaga
The band of Iroquois broods on what is lost
As Mohammed Iqbal mused in Sicily
And wept Granada's lovely rise, and fall.

ST. PETER'S

Out of the great doors flowed the appealing steps
Like a tongue of love, sucking me in.
I had travelled far. It was easy to say yes.

The huge interior opened fearful depths.
I crawled into the caverns and was lost.
The infinite spaces made me crave a guide.

But as the black frocks rushed to shepherd me
One lonely woman knelt down on bare stone
And the whole vast ruin shrank to marble paint.

FINIS THE CENCI

Beatrice, on the high wooden throne,
Surveys the crowded square, the priests, the cross
Before her eyes. She kisses Christ's five wounds.

Beside her, as a sign, her mother's head
Bleeds in the dust. Her brother waits his turn.

She does not let
Those hands approach, but lays aside
Her veil and bodice in so swift a throw
That not a girlish breast is seen
By all the staring multitude
Before she floods her mother.

This is her public modesty, who knew
A father's rape
A father's eye
The driven nail
Her father's blood.

Later they slowly crushed her brother's bones.

THE SEED THROWER

The street-sounds of Delhi, the swirl
Of colour and caste, endless and random,
Did not disturb him as he sat on the ground
In the small circle of his skill.

A green bird perched on his forefinger.

He threw a seed in the air, and the quick wings
Flashed upward till beak caught the tiny prize,
Flew for an instant freely overhead,
An age-old anecdote of India,
Then, folding, fell to sudden stop
Upon the waiting hand.

The bird was safe again. A small green bird.

One day I tossed into the living air
Something you rose to take for nourishment,
Something that bore you upward and beyond,
But I had folded both my hands away
And saw you fading, fading in the sky.

EVOLUTION

This is the monsoon season. Insects, beetles and bugs
Penetrate the loose-fitting screen and take over my room,
Some crawling painfully slowly over the carpet
Their wings closed, their tentacled feet caught in the pile,
Trying desperately to adapt to the strange ground,
Others zig-zagging like rising kites till they hit the wall
       that should not be there.
Most, frantic within the hot dazzle of the lampshade,
Achieving fearful ecstasy and delirium, a total disorder.

Astonishing soil of Burma! Outside
Are those that cannot get in, their blind movement
Not having located the chance openings, yet they too
Are turned from their nuptial flight by man and his glare.
Are driven toward him, cannot leave him alone,
Though millions of selected gradations led to this mating moment.
Here is power more potent.

Variety, variety! On the same night,
In the same country and climate, in an acre range,
Flourish the multiple species. Wings and no wings,
Covered wings and open wings, paired single or double,
And the transient Icarus wings
That fall off in flight, wafted like dust on the roadway.
Yet all are fit to survive since they have survived
Under an equal rain and identical sun.

Uneasy Darwin! Too many are fit to survive,
But only within a balance my needs can destroy.
I turn back to my typewriter. On the key of I
Is a small green speck, which suddenly
          jumps.

ON KANBAWZA ROAD

In Southeast Asia
  the Buddhist New Year
    starts with a water festival
      lasting for days

Everything is put aside
  for this glorification
    of rebirth

Even the guerrillas
  who regularly cut the water-main
    into Rangoon
      promised no damage to the pipe-line
        during these celebrations

Only astrologers can tell
  the exact moment
    when the god descends
      and the year is born

A gun booms out their message

And walking by the Kanbawza Hotel
  on that bright morning
    under a torrid sun

I approached a gate on the roadway
  where stood a girl-child
    not three feet high
      holding a bowl of water
        with a spray
          of the sacred tha-bye tree

She too was celebrating
  she was waiting to sprinkle
    each passerby
      with the symbolic drops

But I   I was a white man
   standing so far above her
      not easy to anoint

She moved toward me
   then drew back
      afraid

She understood the ritual
   taught in her family
      but never dreamed a foreign giant
         might need her blessing

Seeing her torn
   between faith and fear
      I sat down on my heels
         Burmese fashion
            levelling my eyes with her eyes

At once her fear vanished
   she smiled at me
      her little hands
         dipped the sprig in the bowl
            and touched me with the fertility of love

BANGKOK

Deep in the brown bosom
Where all the temples rose
I wandered in a land
That I had never owned
With millions all around.

I had been here before
But never to this place
Which seemed so nearly home
Yet was so far away
I was not here at all.

There was a central mound
That took away my breath
So steep it was and round
So sudden by my side
So Asia all beyond.

And when I came inside
I had to walk barefoot
For this was holy ground
Where I was being taught
To worship on a mat.

A great white wind arose
And shakes of temple bells
Descended from the eaves
To make this gold and brown
One continent of love.

And only my own lack
Of love within the core
Sealed up my temple door
Made it too hard to break
And forced me to turn back.

WATER

And if I ask, you shall bring me water.
It will be cold, first, as it comes clear
Out of a granite pool in the northland,
Single as metal, and as metal, clean.

But this will not suffice.
This is escape water.

So you shall fetch me water from a tap
That has been tunnelled, filtered, piped and drawn,
Civilized water, doctored for man's use,
Tax-paid, civic and obligatory.
Of this water are Empires built,
Trade flourishes, and God is secure.

This is general water. I am easier now,
Knowing an order in the universe.
I will stay awhile with this water,
But not too long. You are not excused.

Go now and find the water that men await
With thirsty cattle under a blazing sun
While earth cracks
And thin streams run dry,
The precious, prayed-for and uncertain water
Of arid lands where men are wandering.
Or bring the sister water, warm and green,
Reeking with life and fetid from the swamp
Whose scum flows slowly under a hum of flies.
Bring me this rare, this livid water,
Tribal water, controlling water,
Charged full of politics and power and race.

Here now is challenge water. I am free.
Here is a glass of liquid for the hand,
A man may drink his fill of, and be well.

of this poem in its favour, though it shares
in my totality. Like adverbs, it qualifies
that to which it is attached, adding
slowly, carefully, painfully, to my living.
Hosts pay for dinner though the guests
be uninvited, and symbiosis
is seldom equal. What most impresses me
is its immortality, and the "bigness of its littleness."
Truly a marvel of adaptation, equally at home in ponds or paunches
since the beginning of life, and a threat to religion, with
an ancestry older than all the gods. Not being oviparous,
and multiplying geometrically by diffusion of fission,
parent and child are the same. Such a conception
is wholly immaculate, needing no redemption.
Hence no one is born at the expense of another
and death is purely external, an accident
but not a law. Then, as its size
is the reverse of colossal, it seems as far removed
as a prowling space-ship, thus creating
a vastness and mythology in my internal universe
which makes me macroscopic. Too long
have the surfaces sufficed us. Beauty, we are mistaught,
is skin deep, and holy men, lonely in caves,
have tried to resist temptation
by dwelling on the viscera of women,
thus spitting at heaven and bespattering themselves.
I proclaim equal rights for the parts, the wonder
of interdependence, the worth
of the cellular proletariate whose ceaseless labour
builds the cathedrals of eyes and hands. I honour
the encyclopaedia of the pseudopodia. The I of the self
is no less in them than in the entire colony, for individuality
lies beneath collectivity. But as to a relationship
unsought by either side, there is need
for bio-justice. None need tolerate
invasion of frontiers, bacillary insurrections,

unicellular anarchy, though such zeal
be without evil. I am its good, it is not mine, and herein lies
the right of defence. Therefore though I praise
this protozoic ancestor,
I aim at its death with all my feeble weapons,
knowing I do not know if it still survives.

A GRAIN OF RICE

Such majestic rhythms, such tiny disturbances.
The rain of the monsoon falls, an inescapable treasure,
Hundreds of millions live
Only because of the certainty of this season,
       The turn of the wind.

The frame of our human house rests on the motion
Of earth and of moon, the rise of continents,
Invasion of deserts, erosion of hills,
       The capping of ice.

Today, while Europe tilted, drying the Baltic,
I read of a battle between brothers in anguish.
       A flag moved a mile.

And today, from a curled leaf cocoon, in the course of its rhythm,
I saw the break of a shell, the creation
Of a great Asian moth, radiant, fragile,
Incapable of not being born, and trembling
       To live its brief moment.

Religions build walls round our love, and science
Is equal of truth and of error. Yet always we find
Such ordered purpose in cell and in galaxy,
So great a glory in life-thrust and mind-range,
Such widening frontiers to draw out our longings,
       We grow to one world
       Through enlargement of wonder.

JAPANESE SAND GARDEN

                    raked
        in long lines   by bamboo prongs
                    white sand
            endless   a distance

                    small rocks
                    islands
            here three   here two
                    and faraway
            three   two   two

                    around them
                    the prongs
                make sand-circles
                waves breaking

            in their stone clefts
                    moss
                    river deltas

                    the farther
                    the smaller

                    suddenly
                horizons vanish
                in this vast ocean
                where the most
            is made from the least
        and the eternally relative
                    absorbs
            the ephemeral absolute

JOURNEY

I travelled around the world
And saw great temples and tombs
Standing on mounds of time
Where nations had come and gone.

Karnak, Parthenon, Rome,
Angkor, Téotihuacán,
Abandoned on the road
As the inner spirit died.

Out of deep silence, a word,
A single aim, a new creed;
A king who is God, or a sword
Hung over every head.

Move out and let me in
Cry the nations, one to one,
Your God's kingdom is down,
Now it is my God's turn.

As a snail, at a snail's pace
Starts on its short trek,
Dies in a last shock,
And leaves the tower on its back,

So the faith of an age gave birth
To these shells, now empty,
Save for the old far sound
Of tides in this human sea.

VI
Insights

BOOKS OF POEMS

Each waits his turn to speak. They lean
And draw upon each other for support,
Their dust-covers making bright signals
Like skirts on girls before they start to dance.

At night they send their meaning through a room
By a hidden movement and a breath
Of penetration, as from outer space
Mysterious powers pierce us with their rays.

Lying awake, I share the immense
Pain of the heart, the burning sight and insight
That broke the walls of silence, to give back
So much of human triumph and despair
Onto this trembling air.

The white of their pages is pressed as close
As dust on settled bones, and wraps them now
In their stilled ecstasy.
                    I choose, and read,
And find beyond their *Deaths and Entrances*
Their grief, their joy, their passion, and their song.

À L'ANGE AVANT-GARDIEN

We must leave the hand rails and the Ariadne-threads,
The psychiatrists and all the apron strings
And take a whole new country for our own.

Of course we are neurotic; we are everything.
Guilt is the backstage of our innocent play.
To us normal and abnormal are two sides of a road.

We shall not fare too well on this journey.
Our food and shelter are not easy to find
In the *salons des refusés*, the little mags of our friends.

But it is you, rebellious angel, you we trust.
Astride the cultures, feet planted in heaven and hell,
You guard the making, never what's made and paid.

POETRY

Nothing can take its place. If I write "ostrich,"
Those who have never seen the bird see it
With its head in the sand and its plumes fluffed with the wind
Like Mackenzie King talking on Freedom of Trade.

And if I write "holocaust," and "nightingales,"
I startle the insurance agents and the virgins
Who belong, by this alchemy, in the same category,
Since both are very worried about their premiums.

A rose and a rose are two roses; "a rose is a rose is a rose."
Sometimes I have walked down a street marked No Outlet
Only to find that what was blocking my path
Was a railroad track roaring away to the west.

So I know it will survive. Not even the decline of reading
And the substitution of advertising for genuine pornography
Can crush the uprush of the mushrooming verb
Or drown the overtone of the noun on its own.

A HILL FOR LEOPARDI

Every day I go up this hill
Onto the lonely plateau
And take off quietly into space.

The traffic and all the trivial sounds
Fade far away. I mount
Swiftly, for time is short, flight beckons
Out where the world becomes worlds, suns pass, galaxies
Shrink and explode, time bends, and motion,
A sweep of laws,
Rolls up all my strength and all
Into one marvel.

Yet it is always the same. A loved voice, a touch,
A phone ringing, and the thrust dies.
Another journey ends where it began
Shipwrecked on ground we tread a little while.

WILL TO WIN

Your tall French legs, my V for victory,
My sign and symphony, Eroica,
Uphold me in these days of my occupation
And stir my underground resistance.

Crushed by the insidious infiltration of routine
I was wholly overrun and quite cut off.
The secret agents of my daily detail
Had my capital city under their rule and thumb.

Only a handful of me escaped to the hillside,
Your side, my sweet and holy inside,
And cowering there for a moment I drew breath,
Grew solid as trees, took root in a fertile soil.

Here by my hidden fires, drop your supplies –
Love, insight, sensibility, and myth –
Thousands of fragments rally to my cause,
I ride like Joan to conquer my whole man.

DEVOIR MOLLUSCULE

Make small and hard,
Make round, distinct and hard
These verities that hammer and intrude
Upon the careless fringes of the heart.
O leave not these sharp grains
Without their shell of lustre and allure.

MEETING

If what we say and do is quick and intense,
And if in our minds we see the end before starting,
It is not fear, but understanding, that holds us.

My dear, my nearly darling, at the beginning
We had already been there, and so did not need to go.
The new to be had is not all we would have in the having.

What has not been taken, stays, and what stays
Is shared in the not taking. We are surrounded
By forms that are substantial, and the symbol
Runs out to greet us as we pass it by.

Such is our world, we cannot be contained
In our fathers' houses. We both have moved
Beyond the classic pattern. Though the direction
Escape us, we are not lost, for we have both
Shared in the searching.

HARDEST IT IS

Your touch is a torch,
A bruise, the spirit broken,
Slow movement under an arch,
The sea's interminable motion.

Touching falters, too long extended,
Touching quickens, infinitely withheld.
Between hard and harder lies the ecstasy.
Hardest it is to touch yet have and hold.

UNION

Come to me
Not as a river willingly downward falls
To be lost in a wide ocean
But come to me
As flood-tide comes to shore-line
Filling empty bays
With a white stillness
Mating earth and sea.

UNISON

What is it makes a church so like a poem?
The inner silence – spaces between words?

The ancient pews set out in rhyming rows
Where old men sit and lovers are so still?

Or something just beyond that can't be seen,
Yet seems to move if we should look away?

It is not in the choir and the priest.
It is the empty church has most to say.

It cannot be the structure of the stone.
Sometimes mute buildings rise above a church.

Nor is it just the reason it was built.
Often it does not speak to us at all.

Men have done murders here as in a street,
And blinded men have smashed a holy place.

Men will walk by a church and never know
What lies within, as men will scorn a book.

Then surely it is not the church itself
That makes a church so very like a poem,

But only that unfolding of the heart
That lifts us upward in a blaze of light

And turns a nave of stone or page of words
To Holy, Holy, Holy without end.

DIALOGUE

The skin is bare for union,
And spirit takes communion
From every living touch.
The skin is bare for union.

The sense is more than mortal.
Our bodies are the portal
Of all created worlds.
The sense is more than mortal.

The eye perceives the token,
The ear the wonder spoken,
The hand is mind's disciple.
The eye perceives the token.

All life embraces matter,
Compelling parts that scatter
To house a new conception.
All life embraces matter.

Desire first, then structure,
Complete the balanced picture.
The thought requires the form.
Desire first, then structure.

Nor seed, nor soil, are single.
Too close the forces mingle,
Too intimate the bond.
Nor seed, nor soil, are single.

For us, how small the power
To build our dreams a tower
Or cast the molten need.
For us, how small the power.

So few, so worn, the symbols.
No line or word resembles
The vision in its womb.
So few, so worn, the symbols.

TO —

You are my cloudless peak
You are my summit talk
Above the lesser hills
You are my Everest

SIGNATURE

On the cold, the November, ground
We bared the warmth of our wound,
And on a most leafless scene
Poured forth our evergreen.

Our love clashed with the wind,
Carved tokens on ice, and signed
Over that northern fact
The consummate, personal pact.

MESSAGE

If words can drop like rain from trees
And speak of love, as rain can speak,
Then these my words shall fall from trees
And speak our love as rain once spoke
Under the overarching leaves.

We lay, twin divers, on the grass,
As in some pool the salmon wait
Until the slender streams amass
A flood of water, and the spate
Opens the narrows, and they pass.

Some wood-paths lead beside a lake
Lonely with sun and shored by hills
Where, tenants of one room, we take
A sky of love, immense, that fills
Heart to the brim, too brief to break,

And some lead outward from the wood
Dropping to roads and planted fields
Where houses stand whose quiet mood
Of love is seasoned. He would lose
In choosing, what he did not choose.

DEPARTURE

Always I shall remember you, as my car moved
Away from the station and left you alone by the gate
Utterly and forever frozen in time and solitude
Like a tree on the north shore of Lake Superior.
It was a moment only, and you were gone,
And I was gone, and we and it were gone,
And the two parts of the enormous whole we had known
Melted and swirled away in their separate streams
Down the smooth granite slope of our watershed.

We shall find, each, the deep sea in the end,
A stillness, and a movement only of tides
That wash a world, whole continents between,
Flooding the estuaries of alien lands.
And we shall know, after the flow and ebb,
Things central, absolute and whole.
Brought clear of silt, into the open roads,
Events shall pass like waves, and we shall stay.

PRISON

In Fullum Street gaol
In the nineteen hundred and fiftieth year of the Christian era
Insane women, locked in filthy cells,
Scream and howl unattended.
(See the Montreal *Herald* for February the second.)
At the Ritz the Bach Partita
Is the more exquisite because it can come
Out of such a world.
I too scream in my cell,
For my own inattention
Built their gaol, my prison,
In the far reaches of the inner mind.

WINDFALL

Until this poem is over, I shall not leave
This leaf, held like the heartache in my hand,
Fallen from brave contagion of the sun,
Fallen from branches wounded by a wind
And resting, now, as green as when it flew
With sap in the stalk and veins stiff with show.

This small complete and perfect thing
Cut off from wholeness is my heart's suffering.
This separate part of something grown and torn
Is my heart's image that now rests on stone.

This is a leaf I talk to as a lover
And lay down gently now my poem is over.

RETURN

Bolder than brass, and brazen in our bed
We mine the stripped veins of our own sub-ground,
Test heart's amalgam, and in the earthy wound
Unloose the molten and imprisoned flood.
Then colder through the mountain of our pride
We shoot our shafts into the central ore,
Our pick our pluck, our wage the love we share,
Our royalty the richness of our lode.

One time you heard upon the outer air
Your freedom calling, and you turned and fled
Up the long pathway of your own descent
To the lip of the world, your hand upon the door,
But stopped too soon, looked round at the way you went—
Eurydice, drawn back by the deeper blood.

A MOVING PICTURE

In the dry days of March
When the snow was dismayed
And the year at its ebb
I drank of my drug
And stared at the screen
Content to be lulled.

I thought I was dead
In the rooms of my heart
So busy the hours
The minutes all full
The mind so engaged
I scarce looked beneath.

Till a river in flood
Rolled over its rocks
And out on the beach
The sand was all smooth
No footmarks were seen.

What came from the dark?
What moment returned
When a girl played her part
Unknown in her role
By the banks of a stream
And you came alive
In the rooms of my heart?

Then suddenly trees
Spoke out of their truth
The ways of our love
The laws of the earth.

On the edge of a field
A circle of grass
Where lovers had lain
Close under a wood

Stared up at the sky
A circle of grass
Where once we lay down
So long, long ago.

SONG

As she lay in my arms
   weeping, weeping,
knowing me far
   beyond reach of her keeping,
what could I say
   as her heart lay breaking
when the root of her sorrow
   was not of my making?

I could only say, Darling
   once I, too, was grieving
for deep in my anguish
   my true love was leaving,
and this is the prison
   that lovers must enter
who give up their freedom
   in search of their centre.

FULL VALLEYS

Fly away, away, swallow,
  Summer is done.
Time to be gone, swallow,
  Time to be gone.

No swifter your flight than the flight
  Of warm days,
Less sudden of pain to the heart
  Than memories.

Only a fat bee crawling
  Over dry grass
Speaks of the droning and humming
  When August was.

Only the fall of a leaf
  On brown ground
Whispers of greener life
  When the heart burned.

And I would be alone now
  Under the slanting sun
Building a world of my own
  Out of things that are gone –

The first loves, and the hates,
  The spur and the goal, the hurt
Of wound and of wounding, the bright
  Roads of the heart.

For in these final days
  Long silences
Are of old words and ways
  Full valleys.

KEEPSAKE

Take these remembrances I leave with you
Momentarily, for their days' use and flavour.
Your mother would have folded them away
In a rubbed album or an inner drawer.
You prefer a casual glance and the waste-basket.

Because we have looked out of the same window
I shall always be behind your eyes
Sharpening unexpected features of your landscape.

To see the world differently because of me
Is your only keepsake
And my afterwards.

EXCURSION

It might have been a say-so, a memory, or mere good will
Hidden under the forms of love,
For who knows when he begins this journey
What he will find to be true?

Everything seems the same when we start —
The station, the train at the platform,
Friends we have known so long waving goodbye
And the sense that we have left something behind.

But that is not what happened at all.

This day there was a change in the line
And suddenly it was the other side of the hills,
A sharp descent, the fronds, the dissolving sea.

THE SPRING VIRGIN CRIES AT HER CULT

The sonlight of her sun shone through her pain
As she knelt on curling shoots in the mounded earth,
And she was the pillar and portico of fanes
Whose crowds of worshippers were come to
    christening.

She pressed a thumb and moved into the ground
And in the warmth and farther down she swam
Till black was darker than the framing soil
And fruits were swelling upwards as they burst
Underneath, overhead, rooted in seeds and birds.

"Dear God O god this is no prayer of mine
That sons be unto me as sun to you.
I have been planted but I am not sown
And the arches of my seasons are taller than the hands
    of your priests."

Her bodiness grew solider than stone,
More central than where spinning poles must meet.
Her skin was land, her eyes the full-blood seas,
And the rapture she would contain was the round,
    red world.

INVERT

Casting about for love, when his eye rested, even for a moment,
His longing poured forth a whole cathedral of worship and prayer
Over the miraculous cause of his conversion.
Up went the pillar and the arching roof
While lights flared in the chancel, and a boy at the altar
Offered a single candle to the Madonna.
But always he came away with his own lost soul
Wrapped round the cold stone fact he would not face
Till, lonely amid the flux, his ego turned
And creeping back upon its source, was left
Beside its own true love, himself, in the crypt of his heart.

NOCTAMBULE

Noctambule, the mode of night,
Leaf-lover lane, and day soon breaking.
Chance meeting, tenderer,
Of casual splendour, blended and ended.
Not best, but only one, hold on then,
Choice comes sudden and swift with departure.
Symphony is lonely, take overture.
Build on beginnings, try now and test for the splendid.

ADVICE

Beware the casual need
By which the heart is bound;
Pluck out the quickening seed
That falls on stony ground.

Forgo the shallow gain,
The favour of an hour.
Escape, by early pain,
The death before the flower.

YOURS

It lay unfolded upward on my knee
Armed five wise ways like Shiva for the dance,
Cross-lined for life, for love, for coming fate,
Warm, as I matched it with my own right hand.

REVERIE

If you were to walk now
From any fireplace to any window,
I know how you would walk.
And if you were to say, seeing the light failing,
"Night never seems to come too soon,"
I know how your words would carry across a room.

But who now sees you walk, or hears you speak,
I do not know,
Nor whether they watch you, moving,
Or hear with the heart the woman-tone of your words.

BOOKWORM

Stand still upon the stairway
And lean your head upon the banister
While I count the moments till you move.
You shall be *La Figlia Che Piange*,
And I – T.S. Eliot the sentimentalist.
Let us cast over this natural event
The drapery of a literary allusion.

TO JOAN

Mist hung in the valley, birds stilled, and the dusk
Drew a cool cloak around us as we bent
To pick her summer flowers. We had been sent
Into her Townships garden, now a husk
Of emptiness, the meaning driven away
By a red cancer crowding on a heart,
And Nature, that had played this double part,
Seemed to have lost her glory and her sway.

Yet we chose careful messengers that hour,
Pinks, gladioli, roses – her own choice,
To place a moment by her other bed.
This was her making, these the words she said,
And she shall hear once more their happy voice
As she dies back to earth like any flower.

HEART

Heart goes straight on,
Heart can't turn.
Mountains won't stop heart.
Drives right in.

Heart can't see a fact
Staring it in the face
If heart loves face.

Heart believes in miracles,
Being miracle.

Magnet heart draws loose ends
Into strict line,
Sews patches up
With no join.

Though heart knows heart breaks
When it fastens,
Stubborn, this part!
Never listens.

PLACE DE LA CONCORDE

Love is a city
               loving is a thorough
                                   fare
            lovers are a populace
               each to each a crowded street
               so much happening
               and passing
      windows of wonder and colour where it is holy
                     to stroll
         to discover
                        doors domes the white façade
                        intersections and little lanes

               O Arch of Triumph
               Notre Dame de Bon Voyage

The city of love sleeps
                        hardly at all
               every road
            leads to the centre
         the traffic pours into a *rond point*
               turning slowly
            and it takes time
                           to melt away

Three bells sound from a church
               lovers know it is a worshipping
               a holding aloft till
                  it is finished
               and they are free to
                        go

The city of love is
                    two cities
            divided by a river wide
                        as lovers are apart
            two banks
                        and walks by water
                different
            an element between

If the bridges stand
            if they are old and beautiful
        if underneath
                        there is the to and fro
            it is one life that is led
                on both sides
            and only one name is given this city
        for it is always
                    a place
                            of concord.

ON WATCHING MARGARET DYING

Beautiful in death, as the still enveloping flame
Glows into darkness
You touch with invisible rays
Hidden responses of being.
So the cold green light
Rims the northern sky, and the cool
Flow of wind from the hills
Fulfils a Canadian day
When the fields are stripped of their grain
The fireweed red in the clearing
And the first leaves rustle the browning ground.
I have only a heart full
Of the terror and glory of life
For this moment, Margaret,
Before I look away
Torn by the love in your eyes
And watch our turning world
Bury the blaze of this our private sun.

FOR CATHY FISCUS

(Found. after three days' digging. at the bottom of a shaft)

Little Cathy fell, down, down, down the hole in the ground,
The terrible hole, the deep, the narrowing hole,
And stopped the presses in Stockholm and Spokane.
Millions drew to her rescue, dug in their hearts
For that which far, far down lay beyond reach
Of their surface lives, waiting to be brought out.

Cathy, take care, your family that weeps
Is all the men and women of the world
Who have awakened into the pitiless day
And long for you, who are their buried hope,
Your death their dream, your cave their vanished cove.

FOR BRYAN PRIESTMAN

(Drowned while attempting to save a child)

The child fell, turning slowly with arms outstretched like a doll,
One shrill cry dying under the arches,
And floated away, her time briefer than foam.

Nothing was changed on the summer's day. The birds sang,
The busy insects followed their fixed affairs.
Only a Professor of Chemistry, alone on the bridge,
Suddenly awoke from his reverie, into the intense moment,
Saw all the elements of his life compounded for testing,
And plunged with searching hands into his last experiment.

This was a formula he had carried from childhood,
That can work but once in the life of a man.
His were the labels of an old laboratory,
And the long glass tubes of the river.

FOR PEGI NICOL

In the last week of our waiting
She lay on our eyes
And clouded all our days' work.
Yet when it was final
It was as though we had not been forewarned.

She lived her art in her motion and speech
As her painting spoke and moved.
She entered a room like a self-portrait
And her language cut quickly.
Everything that was ordinary became extraordinary
Through her vision and touch,
And what she approached grew bright colours.
She started songs and joys and bells
And gardens of pigeon and children.

Nothing she did was quite finished
Before another need called her,
Yet so advanced on its road
The leaving was victory.

Her writing wove through its grammar
Like a stem through stones,
As when she wrote on her death-bed
"There is an excitement in our kind of affairs
That cannot be compared."

She was a Canadian of these difficult days
When greatness is in our thoughts
And our hands are numb.
Only part of her died.
Her alive is alive.

EPITAPH

(*For Arthur Lismer*)

Where his foot
first went
you freely
now may
walk

It is this
door he
opened

It is your
door

COIL

Coil is a tense
a caged thing
coil is a snake
or a live spring

Coil is a shoot
just broken free
or coil is as huge
as nebulae

And mortal coil
waits, promising
to ease its rage
by uncoiling

WHERE ARE THE CHILDREN?

I sent the children upstairs
Because the grownups were coming.
The grownups stayed too long.

Where, where are the children?

DANCING

Long ago
when I first danced
I danced
holding her
back and arm
making her move
as I moved

she was best
when she was
least herself
lost herself

Now I dance
seeing her dance
away from me
                she
looks at me
dancing
        we
are closer
held in the movement of the dance

I no longer dance
with myself

we are two
not one

the dance
is one

VISION

Vision in long filaments flows
Through the needles of my eyes.
I am fastened to the rose
When it takes me by surprise.

I am clothed in what eye sees.
Snail's small motion, mountain's height,
Dress me with their symmetries
In the robing-rooms of sight.

Summer's silk and winter's wool
Change my inner uniform.
Leaves and grass are cavern cool
As the felted snow is warm.

When the clear and sun-drenched day
Makes a mockery of dress
All the fabric falls away.
I am clothed in nakedness.

Stars so distant, stones nearby
Wait, indifferently, in space
Till an all-perceptive eye
Gives to each its form and place.

Mind is a chameleon
Blending with environment;
To the colours it looks on
Is its own appearance bent.

Yet it changes what it holds
In the knowledge of its gaze
And the universe unfolds
As it multiplies its rays.

Tireless eye, so taut and long,
Touching flowers and flames with ease,
All your wires vibrate with song
When it is the heart that sees.

LAST RITES

Within his tent of pain and oxygen
This man is dying; grave, he mutters prayers,
Stares at the bedside altar through the screens,
Lies still for invocation and for hands.
Priest takes his symbols from a leather bag.
Surplice and stole, the pyx and marks of faith,
And makes a chancel in the ether air.
Nurse too is minister. Tall cylinders,
Her altar-boys, press out rich draughts for lungs
The fluid slowly fills. The trick device
Keeps the worn heart from failing, and bright dials
Flicker their needles as the pressures change,
Like eyelids on his eyes. Priest moves in peace,
Part of his other world. Nurse prays with skills,
Serving her Lord with rites and acts of love.
Both acolytes are uniformed in white
And wear a holy look, for both are near
The very point and purpose of their art.
Nurse is precise and careful. She will fail
In the end, and lose her battle. Death will block
The channels of her aid, and brush aside
All her exact inventions, leaving priest
Triumphant on his ground. But nurse will stare
This evil in the face, will not accept,
Will come with stranger and more cunning tools
To other bedsides, adding skill to skill,
Till death is driven slowly farther back.
How far? She does not ask.
                              Priest does not fight.
He lives through death and death is proof of him.
In the perpetual, unanswerable why
Are born the symbol and the sacrifice.
The warring creeds run past the boundary
And stake their claims to heaven; science drives
The boundary back, and claims the living land,
A revelation growing, piece by piece,
Wonder and mystery as true as God.

And I who watch this rightness and these rites,
I see my father in the dying man,
I am his son who dwells upon the earth,
There is a holy spirit in this room,
And straight toward me from both sides of time
Endless the known and unknown roadways run.

SIGNAL

Always there is light
a monstrance, above an altar,
hidden
by the near fact

the screen of me
and the screen of you
the inside and outside
of a window

I scratch the frosted pane
with nails of love and faith
and the crystalled white opens
a tiny eye
reveals
the wide, the shining country.

BEDSIDE

In June I saw the withering of my mother.
O trees like tears, sweet fellowship of stone!
We moved as one and stared into our hearts
Till night's last round and midnight's courtesy
Was kerchief to our eyes, who found no other.

Our silent strength no help in this assault,
We watched her time creep closer by the hour,
And every lengthened intake, each return,
Brought back some tender moment of her succour.
Each one of us was hers, and none his own.

The root wherein we joined at last uprooted
We lingered, reaching in our shallower soil.
What came before seemed now by time inverted,
The ground I trod was all my former home.

And five no longer integral departed.

REMINDER

Some things surface
Suddenly, without colour –
The old shoe on the snow-pile,
The broken toy in the trash-can,
The bent figure, alone, on the park bench –
Forcing us to look downward
Against the "uplift of art,"
To see ourselves free
From the inflation of greatness,
To face the immediacy
Unfocussed in the heavenward gaze.

POEM FOR LIVING

Bore into
new ore.

Screen the metal
from the rubble.

Put wings
on happenings,

plucking the live moment
from the torrent.

Find the hush
in the onrush.

Free the old
from its mould,

yet be beholden
to the proven.

Use sense
with reticence,

fusing the notion
with the passion.

Avoid flimsy,
or whimsy,

giving gaiety
its moiety.

Genitalia?
Inter alia.

Faster
with no master,

hearing the inner voice
make the choice.

Nothing human
foreign

or small
too small.

Each verse
a universe.

In all ways,
praise.

CARING

Caring is loving, motionless,
An interval of more and less
Between the stress and the distress.

After the present falls the past,
After the festival, the fast.
Always the deepest is the last.

This is the circle we must trace,
Not spiralled outward, but a space
Returning to its starting place.

Centre of all we mourn and bless,
Centre of calm beyond excess,
Who cares for caring, has caress.

VII
Observations and Occasions

CLOTH OF GOLD

The king I saw who walked a cloth of gold,
Who sat upon the throne a child of God,
He was my king when he was most a myth.

Then every man paid homage at his feet.
Some fought his battles and shed ransom blood,
Some slew their rights to magnify his claims.

It was our centuries that cut him down.
Bold kings would totter with the lapse of time.
We pushed them over with our rebel shout.

Yet of this metal are new kingdoms struck.
The unknown kings that filter through the laws
Make baron plans to multiply their fiefs.

We break their shackles but new kings are close.
We smell them in the churches and the schools.
We see their garter on the righteous judge.

And now the corporate kingdoms raise their flags,
Their marriage-contracts stretch their boundaries
And pour their armies into foreign lands.

This clink of gold is echo of a crown.
Father and son are founding dynasties.
Each hailed invention lays a palace stone.

While far across the ploughlands of the East
The single master who is history's dream
Holds up his hand to daze the patient throngs.

It seems the shadow of a king is here
That strides before us to the rising sun,
Some shadow of a king that will not fade.

The tumbled limbs of monarchy are green.
A hundred heads survive our mightiest stroke.
These broken dreams, these fragile interludes. . . .

PAMPLONA, JULY 1969

The huge black bull raced up the street
nostrils flaring
leading the pounding herd
into the skeltering youths
catching one
crushing him again and again against a wall
goring and trampling two others.

This is Spain.

"Assassin! Assassin!" cried the furious crowd
in the afternoon, watching the ignoble sport,
but at the bull, not at the matador!
"Assassin! Assassin!" as facile cleverness
out-tricked the helpless strength.

There the hero stood amid the cheers
master of blood and sand.
Olé, Olé,
the perfect image
of the perpetual Franco.

Elsewhere, that month, men reached the moon.

ECLIPSE

I looked the sun straight in the eye.
He put on dark glasses.

MONARCHY

What a thing is a King
And a Crown
And all the makebelieve around them thrown.
A throne, and throngs, and all their songs and wrongs –
Is this a reign? A sovereign?
All these bands and grand stands?
Is this our life, who live with him we raise
Over all equals? What price our bonnie Prince?
Does he make sense?

Yet if not our own
This throne, who then is all of us?
For we are each and all, not singular
Only, not separate and distinct
But plural, multitudes as one.
So Crown is round and without end or start
As each is universe though only part.

IS

Is
is not the end of
Was
or start of
Will Be
Is
is
Is

WAS

Was is an Is that died
    in our careless hands
and would not stay
    in its niche of time.

We crumble all our nows
    into the dust of Was
not feeling
    the wind blow with us
forgetting Was
    cannot be shaken off
    follows close behind
    breathes down our neck
    guides our reaching hand.

One day we shall look back
    into those staring eyes
and there will be nothing left but
    Was.

WILL BE

My constant guide
Shall Will Be be
Till all my
    Is
    is
    Was

TIME AS NOW

All time is present time.
Present in now
Is all that ever was.
All forces, thoughts, events and spectacles
Having inevitable consequence
Ride the long reaches of on-moving time
And speak their history today in me.
Out of this earth, or out from outer space,
Or out from records in these rocks and books,
Waves flow incessantly,
Their sequel pregnant in our living flesh.
The air I breathe, the neutron in my brain,
This plasma that has ridden fishy veins,
Shape my rehearsing of all former life.
I feel huge mastodons
Press my ape-fingers on this typewriter
Old novae give bright meaning to my words.

SPAN

And there was silence till God spoke.
Two billion years
Before his monstrous mouth
Pronounced its sharp, atomic
                    NO.
Meanwhile life formed, matured
And, hearing,
Died.

COELACANTH

I am an iamb
     because the bones of my social fish
were so precise
       I was meant to be embedded
       in the soft mud of my ancestors
or to be drawn on stone
          giving out words dreams ideas
             regular as ribs
crisp in the perfection of pattern
         dated
       a trilobite in limestone

But the earthquake came
   the sea-bottom cracked
       the floor rose to an island
no time for quiet death
   the tranquillity of fossilization
these were mountain days
   a new language in birds
diaspora of dactyls
   iambs split to the core
     now my ancient frame
cries for the deeps of Zanzibar
    and is answered only by
       I AM

PASSER-BY

Receding footsteps, the endless departure,
They are the years passing, the drip of tears.
On all pavements, away from all doorways,
The linking together of time and our temporal nature.

These that I watched were not of my intimacy,
Having no name and no destination.
A pure form of going into the distance,
But human, and so irrevocable.

We can mark some things with the stone of our carving,
The power to arrest the flow is the artist's power.
We worship Beauty, goddess of reaction,
Freezing our vision into her hardened moulds.

But always the footsteps recede, the stone crumbles,
The tide flows out and does not return.
And from this terror we find no safety in flight
But only in faces turned to the flood of arrival.

MEMORY

Tight skin called Face is drawn
Over the skull's bone comb
Casing the honey brain

And thoughts like bee-line bees
Fly straight from blossom eyes
To store sweet facts in cells

While every branching nerve
Performs its act of love
And keeps our past alive

Within the waxy walls
Lifetimes of sounds and smells
Lie captive in the coils

Till some quick trigger word
Tips off a memory rush
And turns Face bright in a flash

IN TIME OF DOUBT

It was dark
  an Arctic night

People stood fixed
  in their places
      like inuksuits

Time seemed frozen
  no hands moved
    we pointed
        away from each other

All we could do
  was to wait
    in our private silences

Then   yes   truly
  it rose   slowly
    over the horizon

A rim of

Sun

WAITING

I suppose waiting cannot be avoided.
Even a mother waits to bear her child
And a promised bishopric must be confirmed.
Often it's just a matter of fixed time,
Like coming-of-age, or the right to be senator.
But timeless waiting, the uncertain call,
The bell not ringing in the empty room,
Faces at windows, slow retreating steps –
These scissors cut the fibre of our cloth.

Thus waiting for you, prisoner of time,
I saw the place of patience in the world –
The slavish docile sullen empty face
Of backward states and undeveloped tribes,
History's backwash, waiting on unknowns,
Unclaimed deposits, buried moidores,
Old bearded prophets preaching a slow cause.

This other kind, this lurking by a booth,
This one-mast tight-rope you have left me on. . . .

EDEN

Adam stood by a sleeping lion,
Feeling its fur with his toes.
He did not hear Eve approaching,
Like a shy fawn she crept close.

The stillness deepened. He turned.
She stood there, too solemn for speech.
He knew that something had happened
Or she never would stay out of reach.

"What is it? What have you found?"
He stared as she held out her hand.
The innocent fruit was shining.
The truth burned like a brand.

"It is good to eat," she said,
"And pleasant to the eyes,
And – this is the reason I took it –
It is going to make us wise!"

She was like that, the beauty,
Always simple and strong.
She was leading him into trouble
But he could not say she was wrong.

Anyway, what could he do?
She'd already eaten it first.
She could not have all the wisdom.
He'd have to eat and be cursed.

So he ate, and their eyes were opened.
In a flash they knew they were nude.
Their ignorant innocence vanished.
Taste began shaping the crude.

This was no Fall, but Creation,
For although the Terrible Voice
Condemned them to sweat and to labour,
They had conquered the power of choice.

Even God was astonished.
"This man is become one of Us.
If he eat of the Tree of Life...!"
Out they went in a rush.

As the Flaming Sword receded
Eve walked a little ahead.
"If we keep on using this knowledge
I think we'll be back," she said.

BRÉBEUF AND HIS BRETHREN

When de Brébeuf and Lalemant, brave souls,
Were dying by the slow and dreadful coals
Their brother Jesuits in France and Spain
Were burning heretics with equal pain.
For both the human torture made a feast:
Then is priest savage, or Red Indian priest?

RESURRECTION

Christ in the darkness, dead,
His own disaster hid.
His hope for man, too soon
Sealed with the outer stone.

This heaven was at hand,
Men saw the promised land,
Yet swiftly, with a nail
Made fast the earlier rule.

All saviours ever to be
Share this dark tragedy;
The vision beyond reach
Becomes the grave of each.

And that of him which rose
Is our own power to choose
Forever, from defeat,
Kingdoms more splendid yet.

Play Easter to this grave
No Christ can ever leave.
It is one man has fallen,
It is ourselves have risen.

ST. BONIFACE

How shall we not instantaneously love
You, O prairie girl, in the core of your choir,
As your glowing song rings over Winnipeg
In the language of a Quebec village, and longings and centuries,
Farms, orchards, bells and processions
Shine from eyes lit with innocence and pride.
A priest in black conducts you, and a priest
Introduces the evening performance, and a priest
Thanks you on our behalf, and priests
Line the hall as we leave, but your voice
Makes all our Gods sit silent on their thrones
And smile at one another, as though friends.

ON THE TERRACE, QUEBEC

Northward, the ice-carved land,
les pays d'en haut.

South, the softer continent,
river-split.

By Valcartier, three Laurentian hills.
Many years ago, as children,
looking north from the Rectory window
on the longest day of each year
we saw the sun set
in the second dip.

I walk these boards under the citadel,
see the narrow streets below,
the basin, l'Ile d'Orléans,
the gateway.

I think of the English troops
imprisoned in the broken city
in the spring of 1760
waiting the first ship.

Whose flag would it fly?

And that other army, under de Lévis,
victorious at Ste. Foy,
still strong,
watching too.

Suddenly, round the bend,
masts and sails
begin to finger the sky.

The first question was answered.

LA RÉVOLUTION TRANQUILLE

(The making of Mirabel Airport)

Goodbye, Ste. Scholastique,
Goodbye, St. Jerusalem,
Your quiet fields and maple groves
Smothered in concrete.

Goodbye, Ste. Monique,
Farewell, St. Janvier,
Your rural roads all carved
By super-highways.

And St. Canut,
And St. Hermas,
Watch the jumbo-jets
Unload their foreign cargoes.

Faster than sound they come
And drop on St. Jérome
A sonic boom.

Adieu, sweet Ste. Thérèse
de Blainville!
Adieu, la Paroisse
de St. Placide!

ALL THE SPIKES BUT THE LAST

Where are the coolies in your poem, Ned?
Where are the thousands from China who swung their picks with
    bare hands at forty below?

Between the first and the million other spikes they drove, and the
    dressed-up act of Donald Smith, who has sung their story?

Did they fare so well in the land they helped to unite? Did they
    get one of the 25,000,000 CPR acres?

Is all Canada has to say to them written in the Chinese
    Immigration Act?

REGINA 1967

On this prairie
  sunlight
    sharp as knives
      cuts slanting lanes
        through dark-edged clouds.

At sundown
  a man's shadow
    is a hundred yards long.

We forget
  the dust that drifted
    the soil gone

and the RCMP
  shooting the hunger-marchers
    who swept across the Rockies
      in a storm of will.

We forget
  the rhythm of drought
    the play of seasons

for the oil-men have come
  and the miners
    opening the ground
      below the reach
        of hammer and sickle.

Financiers for farmers
  a wealth exposed
    a vision lost

History blown away.

TV WEATHER MAN

He draws his fronts
  with a stroke of chalk
    across the satellite face
      of North America

Makes a ballet
  of lows and highs
    giving swift shape
      to all the winds and clouds

No one below escapes no one is left out
  black ghetto and white suburb
    flaming Detroit and fuming Quebec
      swept under the onrush
        of flood-rain or snow storm
      or held sweltering
        in doldrums

A band of cold furies
  from the wings of Hudson Bay
        descends
  to shuddering Florida
while, in the play of seasons
    a heat-wave chorus
  sweeps up from the Gulf of Mexico
    led by a spin of tornadoes

Where now are the frontiers we defend?
  Where are the edges of our villages?
  Bold choreographer, be careful!
Your dances leap across our loves and hates
  ignore our barriers
    making us doubt
  how long our walls will hold.

YES AND NO

YES opens to the sky its asking arms
And funnels to an I
Cascades of joy.

But crooked NO keeps poking with his nose
A blinding zero.
                    Round and round he goes.

NEWS REPORT

A woman and her child
were found drowned
in Lac des Sables.

A very small notice
in the press.

Having no employment
she had gone to ask help
from her parish priest
but he told her
to come back
the next day.

There was no next day.

The manner of drowning was not given.

The report stated, however,
that she had been
"under psychiatric care"
so no one felt any personal
responsibility.

BASEMENT RESTAURANT

With fishy stare I watch sidewalk strollers
Above my window-table, idling past.
Two pairs of shoes pause in a double V,
One thick and clumsy, one thin points and heels.

No use. I sit alone and shift a leg,
Have other flesh in mind, plumb the menu,
Wondering in what kinds to take communion
With the good God immanent in every *plat du jour*.

Food into Man: Menu into Muse!
Now soup-plate swims with iridescent thought.
Poems are lurking in these *pommes de terre*.
What is it makes the oyster make the ode?

Or this soft breast of chicken make that cheek?
Bread, meat and wine father love, hope and joy.
In every wafer is the presence real.
It is the farmer sows our crops of words.

INCIDENT AT MAY POND

(For Wassily and Estelle)

I put an ant upon a stick
And put the stick into the pond.
The vessel drifted in the wind
And straightaway I was captive too.

A helpless stowed-away ant scoured
His narrow deck to seek escape.
The ship was banged with mighty force
Upon the tendril of a reed.

It swung, and veered, and hit a stone,
Bounced up and down in ripple wave.
Ant clung aboard with cunning care
And searched the edges all around.

Ten feet from shore ship came to rest
Beside a log that made a dock.
A road was cleared to solid ground
But ant by now had laid a plan.

He leaped into the wavy sea
And swam with contradictory stroke,
Six walking feet upon the film
His Christlike body did not break.

I was enchanted by his skill,
His canny sense of where to go.
I felt exempted from the guilt
Of playing God with someone's life,

When suddenly there was a swirl
Beside his desperate flailing legs.
A minnow we had both forgot
Was lurking furtive underneath.

A second swirl, a splash, a plop,
Then utter silence everywhere,
And little rings of widening waves
Expanded outward to this poem.

HAPPENING AT ALDRIDGE'S POND

("There is no silence upon the earth or under the earth like the silence under the sea." E.J. Pratt)

Ned, Ned,
the tin-can death of the Titanic
did not hurt so much
as the aimless killing
of that eighty-ton fin-back
trapped by the inlet pond
in your Newfoundland.

Ned,
you swam at us
with ocean eyes
from Western Bay
our scuba poet
leading us undersea
to the wonder of whales and ships and bergs.

You opened enormous depths
to human sympathy
but did not reach
your kinfolk of Burgeo
who poured their poisonous shot
into this miraculous mountain of motherhood,

While outside the estuary
another whale
her male and mate
circled to and fro
waiting, knowing.

Patient, it caught
through deep waters
the living signals,
felt
the bond of presence,
something beyond
our modes of hearing,
something that spoke across
the silence under the sea.

CALAMITY

A laundry truck
Rolled down the hill
And crashed into my maple tree.
It was a truly North American calamity.
Three cans of beer fell out
(Which in itself was revealing)
And a jumble of skirts and shirts
Spilled onto the ploughed grass.
Dogs barked, and the children
Sprouted like dandelions on my lawn.
Normally we do not speak to one another on this avenue,
But the excitement made us suddenly neighbours.
People who had never been introduced
Exchanged remarks
And for a while we were quite human.
Then the policeman came –
Sedately, for this was Westmount –
And carefully took down all names and numbers.
The towing truck soon followed,
Order was restored.
The starch came raining down.

PICTURE IN "LIFE"

Here is a child, a small American girl-child, age fourteen,
Who has shot a lion. In Africa.
Far from her home in Morristown, New Jersey.
And she has shot a gnu, a wart-hog, and an elephant.
How shall we deal with her? Sir John Myrtle-Jenkinson
Shot lions in Africa in the days of the British,
But he was building an Empire. It was a man's job,
And he was a man, firm and philistine,
The Rule of Law in the deepest jungle,
And a black tie in a crisis.
Even the lions were proud
To pose with him for the *Illustrated London News*.
His was no idle slaughter, but the planting of the Flag,
The erection of the Cross, and the sale of cotton pants.
But this slip of a girl was on holiday from school.
She had not yet entered grade ten.
She killed innocently, unconsciously, as a tourist
Might stop to buy a postcard of Notre Dame.
She does not understand her summer trip
Dries up the sources of the fabulous Nile
And shoots great holes through all the myths of Europe.

CHASM
(*A Montage*)

I am white
I am black
  my blood
     laced with continents

Your animal eyes
narrow
       watch me

My hands clench

"I cut off your head
 beneath the deep waters
    crimson are the stars"

I plant
my beautiful flowers
    upon this grave of ugliness

The red cry from your heart
flows in all my veins
    it is you   not I   who lives

ORANGERIE

Sprays of white blossom
    open from buds
        on my orange bush,
       with small green fruit
      crowding the same branches
    while four whole oranges gleam
       ready and ripe
        bending their stems to earth
         waiting the fall:
a simultaneity of birth, growth and death.
       Looking more closely
      I saw a tiny ant on a twig
    rubbing his feelers together
      and muttering
"Natural Selection! Natural Selection!"

And then I read in the *Scientific American*
      of that myrmecophile beetle
        Atemeles pubicollis
    spending his summers being fed by
        Formica ants
        who adopt him
      because he secretes a juice
    irresistible to ants, and how
      leaving these hosts
       when winter comes
he moves out to the grass-lands
      to find *Myrmica* ants
    there repeating the process
      of succulent secretion
       so he will be dragged
    to another brood chamber
      where he will be fed
      for another six months,
       and sure enough
      watching the migration
        from nest to nest

I saw a confident beetle
trundling along
muttering
"Survival of the Fittest! Survival of the Fittest!"

IMPRESSIONS

Frozen smiles hiss through the serpent eyes.
Hatred explodes and implodes. The racial spear circles back to the
breast.
In the former garden the looming skyscrapers crush in their shade
the trees laden with apples.
"For me, for me" is the tattooed device needled on the foreheads
of children in schools.
A flannelled vulgarity madisons the tastes of the staring
knob-twisters.
Dramatic TV plays are interrupted by floor-waxing girls, and
bathroom shaves cover the forward pass.
Monkey-paws fist in the bottled nuts: back-bench MPs ride in the
chauffeured legislature.
Drum-dancing versifiers strip-tease their sexual rags.
Behind the bench, a black soutane.
Under the boots and tires of victory's heirs the eyes of the lovely
red-skinned girls weep in the reserve dawn, while an igloo joy
is caught in the RCMP trap.
A tight belt strict on a melting ice-floe.
By and by, right and left, *sens unique*.
*Finie la fanfare royale: un drapeau éclos prime sur le bord du
fleuve.*
Pen-knives taken to towering oaks.
Thimbles to Niagara.

SATURDAY SUNDAE

The triple-decker and the double-cone
I side-swipe swiftly, suck the Coke-straws dry.
Ride toadstool seat beside the slab of morgue –
Sweet corner drugstore, sweet pie in the sky.

Him of the front-flap apron, him I sing,
The counter-clockwise clerk in underalls.
Swing low, sweet chocolate, Oh swing, swing,
While cheek by juke the jitter chatter falls.

I swivel on my axle and survey
The latex tintex kotex cutex land.
Soft kingdoms sell for dimes, Life Pic Look Click
Inflate the male with conquest girly grand.

My brothers and my sisters, two by two,
Sit sipping succulence and sighing sex.
Each tiny adolescent universe
A world the vested interests annex.

Such bread and circuses these times allow,
Opium most popular, life so small and slick,
Perhaps with candy is the new world born
And cellophane shall wrap the heretic.

GIRL RUNNING DOWN HILL

Laugh, laugh, the little red shoes
skipping in hops of two-to-a-foot
flew down the sidewalk clippety-clop
while hands and elbows flapped in the wind

All of a sudden my world gave way
as she pulled me into her field of force
a slide of houses tore up the hill
whirled along by her treadmill steps

I raced toward her by standing still
our bodies caught in an Einstein curve
we halved the distance in equal time
brandishing laws of heavenly size

O come O come, sang the old to the young
as her eyes came glowing in smiles and curls
then she flung all her rush in my wrap-around arms
and our two worlds crashed with hurrah hurray

OPEN HOUSE, McGILL

I stood by the Redpath Library
and watched the thousands of students
opening McGill's 150-year-old House
    students of all races and creeds
none of whom had fought on the Plains of Abraham
      or at the battle of Hastings
        no two dressed alike
  bright with colours as trees in October
     all gazing upward
       into the cool blue sky
cheering the girl and two boys who
          dropped
      from 4,000 feet
    with red-and-white parachutes
exactly upon a small patch of campus grass
    missing the trees and tall buildings
      controlling wind and gravity
        with swinging skill
     and speaking no language
save the language of motion

As they floated down
    we were all lifted
        Up

EXAMINER

The routine trickery of the examination
Baffles these hot and discouraged youths.
Driven by they know not what external pressure
They pour their hated self-analysis
Through the nib of confession, onto the accusatory page.

I, who have plotted their immediate downfall,
I am entrusted with the divine categories,
ABCD and the hell of E,
The parade of prize and the backdoor of pass.

In the tight silence
Standing by a green grass window
Watching the fertile earth graduate its sons
With more compassion – not commanding the shape
Of stem and stamen, bringing the trees to pass
By shift of sunlight and increase of rain,
For each seed the whole soil, for the inner life
The environment receptive and contributory –
I shudder at the narrow frames of our text-book schools
In which we plant our so various seedlings.

Each brick-walled barracks
Cut into numbered rooms, black-boarded,
Ties the venturing shoot to the master stick;
The screw-desk rows of lads and girls
Subdued in the shade of an adult –
Their acid subsoil –
Shape the new to the old in the ashen garden.

Shall we open the whole skylight of thought
To these tiptoe minds, bring them our frontier worlds
And the boundless uplands of art for their field of growth?
Or shall we pass them the chosen poems with the footnotes,
Ring the bell on their thoughts, period their play,

Make laws for averages and plans for means,
Print one history book for a whole province, and
Let ninety thousand reach page ten by Tuesday?

As I gather the inadequate paper evidence, I hear
Across the neat campus lawn
The professional mowers drone, clipping the inch-high green.

GOODBYE TO ALL THAT

Boards of Governors, Trustees, Wardens and Overseers,
Stare out from the prison of your black Cadillacs,
For the Historical Chauffeur is driving you past the University Gates
Where you used to turn in once a month to supervise Higher
    Education.

Your kind founded us, they built us, we are grateful. That era is past.
Now we are waving you goodbye.
Your role in this business is definitely over.
You have nothing to contribute now but delay

The poor scholars are awake at last. They have seen the new vision.
They feel in their probing hands the form of the future.
They know that the evolution of man
Is shaped by the knowledge they accumulate, test and impart.

So let us have no more of this well-meaning interference,
For you cannot escape your conventional outlook
The current stock of accepted slogans that passes for thinking.
The maintenance of your power depends upon it.
You cannot afford to admit the first principle of a university –
That all truth is relative
And only the obligation to search for it is absolute.

AUDACITY

("*Audacity is missing in Canada.*" The *Times* 30/11/59)

They say we lack audacity, that we are middle class, without the
    adventurousness that arises from the desperation of the lower
    classes or the tradition of the upper classes.
They say we are more emphatically middling than any country
    west of Switzerland, and that boldness and experiment are far
    from our complacent thoughts.
But I say to you, they do not know where to look, and have not
    the eyes to see.
For audacity is all around us,
Boldness sits in the highest places,
We are riddled with insolence.

Do you want audacity?
Let me tell you –
Any day in Montreal you may hear the guns crack at the
    noon-hour, as the police give chase to the bank-robbers
Who are helping themselves to the wealth of the land like the
    French and the English before them, *coureur de bois* and
    fur-trader rolled into one;
You may watch the patrol cars circle their beats to gather the
    weekly pay-off from unlicensed cafés
Whose owners sell booze on the side to acquire the $15,000 they
    need for the $25-permit;
You may learn the name of the distinguished Legislative
    Councillor who controls the *caisse-électorale*
Into which rattles the coin that makes possible the letting of
    contracts,
And who tips his hat to the priest
And is saluted respectfully in return;
You may marvel at the boldness of promoters of oil and natural
    gas, men too quick for production, fixers and peddlers,
Getting their hands on concessions and rights, access to
    underground treasures awaiting man's use in the womb of
    our northland,

Playing the suckers and markets, turning their thousands to
    millions, loading the pipe-lines with overhead that is paid by
    the housewife who cooks her spaghetti,
Then solemnly demanding higher rates for sales of the product
    (extra hot, natural gas!) before friends on the Board of
    Control:
You may follow the hucksters and admen compiling their
    budgets, planning the assault on "public opinion," setting the
    poll-questions,
Writing editorials for weeklies, letters to editors, telegrams to
    senators, articles for journals,
Day after day on the job of confusing the issue, baiting the
    eggheads, laughing at the "culture kids" of CBC, fixing the
    give-aways,
Posing as democracy's friends and admirers, while undermining
    the concept of government and welfare,
Singing the praises of free enterprise that relies on high tariffs,
    defence contracts and floor prices;
You may stand in awe at the audacity of journalists, twisting the
    news items by headline and rewrite, blanking out truth,
Ponderously laying down the conventional wisdom in
    unconventional English,
While a few owners gather dailies into chains run by gangs of
    paid hack-men,
Then add on the radio stations and TV outlets, lest some glimmer
    of free opinion escape them;
You may be amazed at the boldness of churchmen and ministers,
    meeting in synod and conclave and conference to spy out our
    sinfulness,
Who wax indignant over lotteries, horse-racing and the drink
    question, or, with Savonarola intensity,
Denounce crime-comics and short bathing-suits;
But all this is as nothing, not worthy of mention,
Beside the supreme, the breath-taking audacity
Of the great executives in their panelled boardrooms
Found at every point in the social structure where policy is laid
    down or decision taken,
Without whom no hospital can be opened, no charitable
    campaign launched, no church can engage a preacher and no
    university can build a building,

Daring to be omniscient, omnipotent, omnipresent, not to
     mention omnivorous –
These surely you can see in this Canada of ours, O London
     Times,
In this country that has the audacity to proclaim the "supremacy
     of God"
In its Bill of Rights?

STUDENT PARITY

The arrogant assurance of an unchangeable certainty
is visible on the faces of these young activists.
The building they have occupied is dedicated to science
but their demands are "not negotiable."

In the fourth-floor genetics laboratory
a skilled researcher is close to a breakthrough on cancer
but his future employment at the University is uncertain
because students have parity on his selection committee
and he has not publicly protested the war in Vietnam.

THIS IS A LAW

Who says Go
When the Green says Go?
And who says No
When the Red says No?
Asked I.

I, said the Law,
I say Go
When the Green says Go
And don't you Go
When the Red says No,
Said the Law.

Who are you
To tell me so
To tell me Go
When the Green says Go
And tell me No
When the Red says No?
Asked I.

I am you
Said the Law.

Are you me
As I want to be?
I don't even know
Who you are.

I speak for you
Said the Law.

You speak for me?
Who told you you should?
Who told you you could?
How can this thing be
When I'm not the same as before?

I was made for you
I am made by you
I am human too
So change me if you will
Change the Green to Red
Shoot the ruling class
Stand me on my head
I will not be dead
I'll be telling you Go
I'll be telling you No
For this is a Law
Said the Law.

ON SAYING GOODBYE TO MY ROOM
IN CHANCELLOR DAY HALL

Rude and rough men are invading my sanctuary.
They are carting away all my books and papers.
My pictures are stacked in an ugly pile in the corner.
        There is murder in my cathedral.

The precious files, filled with yesterday's writing,
The letters from friends long dead, the irreplaceable evidence
Of battles now over, or worse, still in full combat –
        Where are they going? How shall I find them again?

Miserable vandals, stuffing me into your cartons,
This is a functioning office, all things are in order,
Or in that better disorder born of long usage.
        I alone can command it.

I alone know the secret thoughts in these cabinets,
And how the letters relate to the pamphlets in boxes.
I alone know the significance of underlinings
        On the pages read closely.

You scatter these sources abroad, and who then shall use them?
Oh, I am told, they will have a small place in some basement.
Gladly some alien shelves in a distant library
        Will give them safe shelter.

But will there be pictures of J.S. Woodsworth and Coldwell
Above the Supreme Court Reports? The Universal Declaration
Of Human Rights, will it be found hanging
        Near the left-wing manifestos?

And where are the corners to hold all the intimate objects
Gathered over the rich, the incredible years?
The sprig of cedar, the segment of Boulder Dam cable,
The heads of Buddha and Dante, the concretions, the arrowheads,
        Where, where will they be?

Or the clock that was taken from my 1923 air-cooled Franklin?
The cardboard Padlock, a gift from awakened students?
The Oxford oar, the Whitefield Quebec, the Lorcini?
      These cry out my history.

These are all cells to my brain, a part of my total.
Each filament thought feeds them into the process
By which we pursue the absolute truth that eludes us.
      They shared my decisions.

Now they are going, and I stand again on new frontiers.
Forgive this moment of weakness, this backward perspective.
Old baggage, I wish you goodbye and good housing.
      I strip for more climbing.

VIII
Letters From
The Mackenzie River

FLYING TO FORT SMITH

The spread of silver wing
   Lifts us into long lanes of space.
We peer through panes of glass.

The plain of lakes below
   Is bound with bands of green
Fringed by darker green
   Pocked with drops of ponds.

Everywhere
   A huge nowhere,
Underlined by a shy railway.

Snaking brown streams
   At every islanded corner
Widen their reaches
   Leaving blue pools behind.

An arena
   Large as Europe
Silent
   Waiting the contest.

Underground
   In the coins of rock
Cities sleep like seeds.

THE CAMP AT BELL ROCK

The plane was ringed in dust
As we whisked the sandy runway.
Bull-dozers were widening
A strip of weeds and grass.
The skinny trees fell back
Showing their grey stalks,
And leaned in broken ranks.

"Chuck your kit in the truck,"
Said Ralph, the boss on the job.
"Hope you have sleeping-bags.
The camp is down at Bell Rock
Eight miles below Fort Smith.
It's better that way for the boys –
Keeps them tied to their work.
We have the guest-house ready.
Andy'll take care of you; meals
Are at 7.00, noon and 5.00."
So our trip began.

The Slave river rolled past
Downhill to the North,
Running away from America
Yet bringing America with it.

Up at Fort Fitzgerald
Where Mackenzie gummed his canoes
The barges moored to the dock
Were long and flat and black,
And the diesel tug was called Peace.

I dipped my hand in water
That muddies the Beaufort Sea.

That night the radio
Spoke to all the skippers
Of tugs scattered north and south
Over twenty-two hundred miles:
Radium Dew, Radium Yellowknife, Radium King,
And Radium Charles, after Charlie Labine.
They came in from Port Radium, Yellowknife,
From Hay River, Waterways, Aklavik,
Fort Resolution, Fort Simpson,
Giving temperatures, winds and cargoes.
Down to 25 on Great Bear, August 14,
Blowing hard on Great Slave,
Snowing at Norman Wells,
Athabaska fair and clear.

The cargoes speak the language of life:
Muckers for mines, acids for ores,
Barrels of oil and gas, timber and pipe,
Bull-dozers and cranes, fork-lifts and drills,
Tough hardware, and the fuels of power.
Under tarpaulins are boxes of fruit,
Tinned vegetables, baby-food and oranges,
And one big flashy fire-truck,
Like a huge toy, red and hosy,
With siren, axes and nozzles,
A civic triumph for the new Aklavik
On the Delta, location E3.

Walking behind the bunk-house
We saw a great white dog,
Long-haired for cold, feet broad for snow,
Standing firm and friendly,
No husky, but mixed with the breed.
Behind him his ugly mother
Slept, a short-haired bitch,
Brown and patchy, an import,
Half his size, but source of his power.
So it is in the North
Where opposites meet and mate.

FORT SMITH

The town siren went off
And everyone looked for the fire.
Kids from every corner
Bounded like little wolves,
While adults stood around
Grinning at the false alarm
As cars and trucks rolled up
With a grand old fire-pump.
Looking about the crowd
I saw a collar reversed,
The white circle of my childhood,
And a gentle Anglican face
In the modest clergyman's dress.

The Rev. Burt Evans
Picked us out as strangers
And offered to show us around
In his new Volkswagen.
So we shoved aside a baby-crib
And filled up the Nazi car
To explore Canada's colony.
There was the Bank of Commerce
In a new tar-paper bunk-house
Opened six days ago,
The Hudson's Bay Store and Hotel,
Government Offices, Liquor Store,
RCMP Headquarters, Catholic Hospital,
Anglican and Catholic Churches,
The Imperial Oil Compound,
The Barber Shop and Pool Room,
A weedy golf course, the Curling Club,
And the Uranium Restaurant, full of young people
Playing song-hits on the juke-box.

We drove on sandy streets.
No names yet, except "Axe-handle Road."
There was the "native quarter,"

Shacks at every angle
For Slave Indians and half-breeds,
And overlooking the river
The trim houses of the civil servants
With little lawns and gardens
And tents for children to play Indian in.

The Rev. Burt Evans
Stopped his car by a Grotto
Close to the Catholic Church.
Rocks had been piled in a heap
To make a cave for the Virgin.
Flags had been draped across
And benches were neatly placed.
"This has an appeal," he said,
"To the superstitious element in the population,"
And sighed a little, as one might,
Who knew it was not quite cricket.

We climbed down to the Slave
To the rock polished by ice
And the roar of the great rapids.
This is the edge of the Shield —
Eastward, away to Labrador,
Lies the pre-Cambrian rock,
While North and South and West
Stretches the central plain
Unbroken from Gulf to Arctic,
Hemmed in by the western hills.
Three boys came out of a hideaway
And showed us fresh tracks of moose.

Pierre, suddenly challenged,
Stripped and walked into the rapids,
Firming his feet against rock,
Standing white, in white water,
Leaning south up the current
To stem the downward rush,
A man testing his strength
Against the strength of his country.

STEVE, THE CARPENTER

Steve Bard, the carpenter,
Stopped us by his workshop.
"What you boys doin' around?
Goin' down to Aklavik?
Say, that is quite a trip.
Been here all of eight years
And never been to Aklavik!
What kind of camera you got?
Do you like taking pictures?
You come and see my pictures.
I got lots I can show you."

So we went that night to his bunk-house –
One room, a bed and table,
And pin-ups on the wall
(One girl draped in a bathtowel
Showing all her glad tidings).
Out came the careful albums,
Hundreds of family scenes,
Two children at various ages,
Mother, sister and brother,
The little farm back in Saskatchewan,
Queen Elizabeth driving through Edmonton,
And Steve himself, every page.

"It's something to do," he said,
"It's a lonely life for me now.
I tried to get along with the missus
But she made my life a hell.
After a time I quit
Just got out and came up here.
I'll never live with her again.
I got one of them lawyers
To help me with my divorce
But he lifted $6,000 off of me
Taking it all in all.

There's my girls, they're fine looking girls,
I haven't seen them for years,
And I know she turned them against me.
It's a lonely life for a man.
Sometimes I get so lonely I could cry."

Outside the Slave rolled on,
Farther and farther from home.

FORT PROVIDENCE

We came out of Beaver Lake
Into swift water,
Past the Big Snye, past Providence Island,
And nosed our barges into shore
Till they grated on stones and sand.
Gang planks, thrown to the bank,
Were all we had for dock
To drop four tons of freight.

A line of men were squatting
Silently above us, straight
Black hair, swarthy skins.
Slavies they call them, who left
Their name on Lake and River.
None of them spoke or moved –
Just sat and watched, quietly,
While the white man heaved at his hardware.
Farther on, by themselves,
The women and girls were huddled.

Then we saw Father Denis,
Oblate from Rennes, Brittany,
In charge of the only mission.
Young, cheerful, crucifix stuck in his waistband,
He greeted us with friendly warmth.
Would show us the school, his pride.

We had seen the school from far off.
It stood four storeys high,
Grey, square, isolated,
More fortlike than anything in Fort Providence.
In the entrance hall
Walt Disney illustrations for the Kleenex Company
Showed children how to avoid getting colds
By constantly using Kleenex.
The gentle sister in charge,
A Grey Nun from Montreal,

Welcomed us in French.
Priests from France, nuns from Quebec,
Taught Slavies (who still speak Indian)
Grades I to VIII, in broken English.

We walked through the crowded classrooms.
No map of Canada or the Territories,
No library or workshop,
Everywhere religious scenes,
Christ and Saints, Stations of the Cross,
Beads hanging from nails, crucifixes,
And two kinds of secular art –
Silk-screen prints of the Group of Seven,
And crayon drawings and masks
Made by the younger children,
The single visible expression
Of the soul of these broken people.

Upstairs on the second storey
Seventy little cots
Touching end to end
In a room 30' by 40'
Housed the resident boys
In this firetrap mental gaol.

THE RADIUM YELLOWKNIFE

This tug is dedicated
To a single purpose –
Pushing freight in the Territories.
240 tons gross, four-foot draft, 1,200 HP.
She burns diesel oil
Pumped at Norman Wells
And so lives off the land.
Coming up the Mackenzie
With seven barges ahead
Roped by steel cables
She is longer than the Queen Mary.

On Great Bear Lake
Hit by a side wind
She rolls and bounces
Till the deck-hands fall out of their bunks,
(So the Prince went down on Athabaska)
And you hear the bottom scrape
In the lower rapids.

Captain Svierson
A wise old Swede
Strolls the upper deck in his T-shirt
(No braid here).
George Bouvier the Pilot
Is from the local Métis;
His father came from the Red River by canoe
And married into the Lafferty's at Providence.
High cheekbones and deep lines mould a face
As wild and gentle as riverlands seen from a plane.
George Rush, the talkative mate,
Jollies the crew along.
Nobody seems to give orders,
Yet everyone knows what to do,
Especially when Grace Fischer,
Cook and sole woman aboard,
Calls them in to eat.

Mother of nine, looking thirty-five,
She utters her soul in pastry,
And reads long letters from daughters
Who are peopling the world "outside."

NORMAN WELLS

Rounding the upper bend
The river is calm and wide
A slowly moving lake,
A mighty total of streams
That dent the endless banks;
The Horn, Bouvier, Redknife,
Rabbitskin, Blackwater, Redstone,
And the big-mouthed Liard
Joining the central flow.

Now we see tanks of oil
Standing white on the rock
Amid stacks of cans and drums.
The first industrial wealth
Marked by Mackenzie himself —
Power and light and heat
For whatever the uses of man.
Bringing out Yellowknife gold
And the burning ore from Port Radium,
Driving the tugs and planes
And keeping the bureaucrat snug.
Underneath perma-frost
It lies so close to the soil
It films the pools in the woods.

Curving in toward shore
We read on a kind of gallows
In this utterly public land
The words PRIVATE PROPERTY.
Behind is its counterpart:
TRESPASSERS WILL BE PROSECUTED
BY ORDER, IMPERIAL OIL.
Trespassers! In this North!
Man is the absent fact
Man is the aim and need
Man is the source of wealth
But Property keeps him out.
And the Indians wonder, who first
Lived off this very soil
And now are outcast and dying
As their substance is drained away.

Even the whites are in thrall,
For a certain Jimmy O'Brien
Who lost his job with Imperial
And could find no other employment
Was being flown outside
On Imperial's company plane
When the news reached CPA,
Who ordered the plane flown back
Since they had an exclusive charter
To carry all passengers.
Jimmy O'Brien came back
And was left to his own devices.
No one seemed to know
How he got out – if he did.

During the Second War
A pipe over the Rockies
Drained from this shallow field
Twelve thousand barrels a day
When the optimum flow is four.
A bomb on Hiroshima
Saved this Canadian wealth.

234

NORMAN WELLS TO AKLAVIK

We carry our packs to the dock
(Two slippery planks on the mud)
And help the pilot to load
The tiny Beaver plane.
For the risky, uncomfortable flight
Canadian Pacific Airways
Exacts a first-class fare
Plus an extra charge
To prove its monopoly power.
By the time we were all seated
With bags stacked in the aisle
No one could move his legs,
No one had safety belts.

Up we rose from the water
And saw the country unfold
With its swarms of streams and lakes
And its widening patches of moss
On and on and on
Too much for the mind to grasp
Too huge to make sense or scheme
With seemingly nothing to say
But its sheer existent fact
And the eerie, empty song
Of colour and light and space.
Slowly the trees declined
Till the tundra reached to the sky.

Then the weather closed in.
Clouds sank to the banks.
Only in sudden holes
In the sullen sky was the land
Glimpsed in the murk below.
The pilot flew with his eyes
Keeping the river beneath.
When we dropped into Aklavik
There was silence in the plane.

Now Indian and Eskimo watch
The slow, inescapable death
Of this land which has waited so long
For the sentence already pronounced.
America's overspill
Invades the tundra and lakes
Extracting, draining away,
Leaving a slum behind,
Spreading its colour and shape
Like brown water on snow.

But wait! A new city is planned
Across from Aklavik's mud,
Free from the perma-frost,
Set upon solid rock,
Blue-printed, pre-fab, precise,
A model, a bureaucrat's dream.
Here we went to observe
The first Council meeting
North of the Arctic Circle,
The birth of democracy
Swaddled in ancient dress,
Where the Commissioner and nine whites
(Four elected and five named)
Came to ratify laws
Pre-cast in Ottawa.
The two of us, looking on,
With a priest in a black soutane,
And the RCMP in its braid
Were all the public around,
No Indian or Eskimo face.

All was in doubt at the start.
The Mace, where was the Mace?
The massive, Massey Mace
Weighing two hundred pounds?
A most magnificent Mace

236

Fashioned of local stuff,
Indian beads, and the tusk
Of a narwhal, Eskimo stone,
And copper from a Franklin kettle
Set in the crest of a Crown.
Alas, the Mace ran aground
Crossing the Delta flats
In a high-speed motor boat,
Somewhere out in the murk
Where only the musk-rat thrives.

Symbols are magic, and work
As well in idea as in fact.
The Great Seal dropped in the Thames
By a fleeing Jacobite King
Hindered not Parliament,
Nor the lack of the Mace this meet.
For now an obedient voice
Carefully coached in advance
Solemnly rose to speak:
"I move that we proceed
In the absence of the Mace
As if the Mace were here."
Carried unanimously! —
The gap in the ritual
Covered by common sense.

MACKENZIE RIVER

This river belongs
  wholly to itself
    obeying its own laws

Its wide brown eye
  softens what it reflects
    from sky and shore

The top water   calm
  moves purposefully
    to a cold sea

Underneath   its stone bed
  shows sunken rock
    in swirl and surface wave

Suspended
  in its liquid force
    is the soil of deltas

The servient valleys
  reach up to lake and spring
    in clefts of far hills

And shed
  arteries of streams
    that stain the central flood

In spring thaw and spate
  its wide levels
    rise slowly   fall

Like tides
  that start upstream
    and die at sea

A river so Canadian
   it turns its back
      on America

The Arctic shore
   receives the vast flow
      a maze of ponds and dikes

In land so bleak and bare
   a single plume of smoke
      is a scroll of history.

IX
Satire and Light Verse

THE PROBLEM

No problem can be worse than mine,
My state is quite pathetic;
One half my soul's a Philistine,
The other half's aesthetic.

A pendulum, I alternate
Between extreme positions;
Now aiming at the Newdigate,
Now loathing such ambitions.

I long to tread the realms of Art,
Yet cling to ways prosaic.
My spirit is as torn apart
As priest and worldly laic.

The consequence is strange to tell:
My constitution I vex
At lunch, by sipping cool Moselle,
At night, by bingeing five-x.

And when an opera is given
With setting most decorous,
At first I taste the artist's heaven,
And then – I scan the chorus!

But these absurdities are small,
My room relates another:
Large rowing groups adorn one wall,
Madonnas grace the other.

O! would some kindly friend of mine
Mix me a strong emetic
To elevate the Philistine
Or humble my aesthetic.

So might I then, grown truly wise,
These mental troubles throttle,
And reach a golden compromise
Or "mean" – (v. Aristotle).

SWEENEY COMES TO McGILL

(With apologies to Mr. Eliot)

The night's unconsciousness abates
As Sweeney's college day begins.
The fifty-thousand-dollar gates
Give promise of more startling sins.

He treads the shiny marble halls,
Nods at a pink and powdered doll.
A furtive memory recalls
The Mount Royal, Childs, the Capitol.

A waning vertebrate extols
The virtues of forgotten bards,
But Sweeney deals in rigmaroles
Thumbing an oily pack of cards.

"The Greeks achieved the only fame...."
His *Daily* rustles, out of sight,
"And Shakespeare had a moral aim...."
Winks at the flapper on his right.

Obediently he writes, and notes
That someone died at thirty-three,
Then draws a fleet of crazy boats
Over a wide and inky sea.

The urgent, academic ooze
Glazes the round, cherubic eyes,
Till Jew and Gentile interfuse
In one astounding compromise.

The furious games are fought and won,
The Thundering Thousands come and go,
Upon St. James Street shines the sun
And Ottawa reflects the glow.

SWEENEY GRADUATES

Sweeney, a ripe collegiate,
Emits stenography. Content
To write as ragged notes dictate,
He earns an adequate per cent.

The hour is procreant. His mind,
Incapable of further suction,
Gives sudden, fissive birth — a kind
Of protoplasmal reproduction.

He sloughs the academic skin.
The intellectual skirmish ends.
Now may the serious work begin
Of piling up the dividends.

Professor Footnote, D.C.L.,
Sifts truth from error. He conjectures
That Sweeney knows his questions well
Since they are answered from his lectures.

His depelliculative dome
Preponderates with pride, as all
His pet ideas come flocking home
Inviolate, identical.

So Sweeney passes. So they pass
In thousands down the milky way.
Nebuchadnezzar, throned in brass,
Laughs at the prophets' disarray

As educated hordes intrude
On meretricious premises,
And magnates in their magnitude
Dispense the dubious degrees.

SCHOOL FOR DOMESTIC SCIENCE

I

Down oily corridors
Lined with cold horrid doors
Miss Russell trips.
The greyish strips
Of her hair seem like ready-to-lay-on-you whips.
Sings:
>   Not a step farther.
>   Try if you dare
>   To speak to a man!
>   I'll be there, so beware!
Moves creaking on, all shrivelling and wooden,
Like a dry wind over a kitchen garden.
"She's a curious, querulous quean,"
Cry bobbed-haired maidens, tossing heads peach-pretty,
"A nig-nagging, notice-board quean."

II

Bright little seniors don sharp glassy airs,
Set soft bright lips as tight as brassieres,
And all in white rows, like sugary chocolates,
Become soft little downy magistrates.
Sing:
>   Miss Dale, primrose pale
>   Come our culprits. They quail
>   When they learn what their grave peccadilloes entail.
>   Now it's you –
>   Quail too!
From the neat pink president, elate and virginal,
Soft feathery admonishments flutter and fall.
Sentence:
>   You'll wear your uniform, green and crisp as a dollar,
>   All day, with your pretty neck in a stiff white collar.
>   No more long walks before your scrubbing. Instead
>   You'll make an extra senior's downy bed.

246

Montreal is far and hard to reach.
It hangs all ripe and rosy like a peach
For youthful fingers, tired of pots and pans,
Sapolio, gas-ranges, laundry-man's
Job-scrubbing. Out one creeps in wind and rain,
Runs to the Cottage, timidly peeps in.
Sings:

> Sleep, Armstrong, sleep,
> Only the mice creep
> Up your wide, bland stairs.
> Toss no more in the dark,
> The dog's cool bark
> Is a prayer to his paramours.

Expansive puppets percolate self-unction
Beneath a portrait of the Prince of Wales.
Miss Crotchet's muse has somehow failed to function,
Yet she's a poetess. Beaming, she sails

From group to chattering group, with such a dear
Victorian saintliness, as is her fashion,
Greeting the other unknowns with a cheer –
Virgins of sixty who still write of passion.

The air is heavy with Canadian topics,
And Carman, Lampman, Roberts, Campbell, Scott,
Are measured for their faith and philanthropics,
Their zeal for God and King, their earnest thought.

The cakes are sweet, but sweeter is the feeling
That one is mixing with the *literati*;
It warms the old, and melts the most congealing.
Really, it is a most delightful party.

Shall we go round the mulberry bush, or shall
We gather at the river, or shall we
Appoint a Poet Laureate this fall,
Or shall we have another cup of tea?

O Canada, O Canada, O can
A day go by without new authors springing
To paint the native maple, and to plan
More ways to set the selfsame welkin ringing?

TOURIST TIME

This fat woman in canvas knickers
Gapes seriously at everything.
We might be a city of the dead
Or cave-men
Instead of simple town folk.
We have nothing to show
That cannot be seen better somewhere else,
Yet for this woman the wonder does not cease.

Madam, the most extraordinary thing in this town
Is the shape of your legs.

O communication!
O rapid transit!

TELEOLOGICAL

Note, please, the embryo.
                    Unseeing
It swims into being.
Elan vital,
Thyroid, gonads *et al.*,
Preserve the unities.
Though endless opportunities
Offer, arm joins shoulder.
Ego forms.   It grows bolder,
Meets fellow anthropoids
In cell-groups.   Avoids
Behaviour that's odd –
Like questioning God,
Not playing games, writing tales,
Or being natural with females.
Leaves home.   Gets ambitions.
Works hard in positions.
Takes to golf.   Makes contacts.
Drops theories for facts.
Always fills in cheque-stubs.
Becomes president of clubs.
Creates a ripple, disturbs particles,
Manufactures articles.
Occupies a front pew
In *Who's Who*.
The Oxford Group
Knocks him for a loop.
At death the estate
Is admittedly great.
Friends knock off work for hours
To see the funeral and flowers.
Who, who shall deny it a name,
Or cry shame
When it makes the discovery
Of the ovary?
Who can prove the illusion
Against the glow of fusion?

DECAY OF CLERIC

Asexual saprophytes unfold
Their sporophores afresh
And propagate a glaucous mould
On penitential flesh,

While choughing worms debate a deed
Too dismal to be borne
And swallow particles of creed
To keep their gizzards warm.

Sarcoplasm, fibroblast,
Fibrins and chromosomes
Now expiate a priestly past
In Non-Conformist homes.

EPITAPHS

FINANCIER

There are poor worms most anxious to take shares
In every one of this great man's affairs.
So shed no tear at this forced liquidation:
It simply means a new incorporation.

LAWYER

His first anxiety appears to be
That he's a client to posterity;
His second that he must, to be forgiven,
Plead his own case before the bar of heaven.

PROFESSOR

This seer lived among the clouds
But not of these are made his shrouds,
For death at last, with solemn mirth,
Has brought him safely down to earth.

TWO SONNETS FOR FREE ENTERPRISE

I
COMPANY MEETING

The Chairman called the proxies to order at ten
And opened proceedings with a short greeting.
The Secretary read the minutes of the last meeting.
The Vice-President doodled with a ball-pointed pen.
The financial statement, including dividends, was adopted.
It was shown that a chief competitor was in liquidation.
So somebody suggested a larger charitable donation.
Then the entire Board was re-elected, with two co-opted.

So the meeting adjourned. Let it adjourn.
Disturb not these High Priests at their ritual magic
Lest unbelief should water the national stock.
The inverted pyramid could so easily overturn
We must keep our mumbo-jumbo. It would be tragic
If this church were found not to be built upon rock.

II
AD-MEN

Take a look at the *Sat Eve Post*,
Get a load of its thick slick ads
That have turned our ancestors into Mums and Dads
And reduced living to the level of making toast.
Have an eyeful of its long slim girls
Selling themselves with lipstick and whiskey and cars
To any man whose distinction is drinking in bars
Using a dictaphone, or buying false pearls.

Hail to the Ad-Men! Knights errant of our time!
Proudly they ride to war for the barons of soap,
Perpetually storming the castles of the home.
This gives our bathrooms a touch of the sublime
So be not discouraged, never give up hope,
And please – no escaping to Moscow or to Rome.

253

COMMAND OF THE AIR

This sweet music that I hear,
Is it Soap, or is it Beer?
Do I owe the string quartet
To Foulness of the Breath, or Sweat?
When the Chopin Prelude comes
Will it help Massage the Gums?
And will Serkin play encores
Mixing Bach and Baseball Scores?
Damn! They've cut the Brahms finale!
Your world's my world, Mr. Dali!

BIG CAMPUS

Twenty thousand boys and girls
Here pursue higher learning.
The disc-jockey's audio-sexual aids
Provide a soft contraceptive jelly
In which Aristotle swims like a baffled spermatozoon.
Flitting in and out of the huge buildings
Little teachers with scared faces, carrying note-books,
And muttering in a strange language
Seem only to darken the flood-lit car-parks.
Steam shovels in every vacant corner
Dig graves for another twenty thousand
Who even now, not waiting for the answers,
Are streaming out of every confident womb.

THE CALL OF THE WILD

Make me over, Mother Nature,
Take the knowledge from my eyes,
Put me back among the pine trees
Where the simple are the wise.

Clear away all evil influence
That can hurt me from the States,
Keep me pure among the beaver
With un-Freudian loves and hates,

Where my Conrads are not Aiken
And John Bishop's Peales don't sound,
Where the Ransoms are not Crowing
And the Ezras do not Pound.

BONNE ENTENTE

("One man's meat is another man's poisson." A. Lismer)

The advantages of living with two cultures
Strike one at every turn,
Especially when one finds a notice in an office building:
"This elevator will not run on Ascension Day";
Or reads in the Montreal *Star*:
"Tomorrow being the Feast of the Immaculate Conception,
There will be no collection of garbage in the city";
Or sees on the restaurant menu the bilingual dish:

DEEP APPLE PIE

TARTE AUX POMMES PROFONDES

THE FOUNDING OF MONTREAL

The boats drew closer to the wooded shore.
The red men stared behind their rim of trees.

Out leapt bold Maisonneuve with sword and flag.
The red men waited on their chieftain's word.

A moment hung prolific on the air.
Culture was straining at its leaden leash.

The shrub I crouched in was my cedar bush
Hung with my future bitter-sweet of love.

And I could see through centuries of glass
Old Arnold Toynbee reaching for his pen,

Saw wigwams sprouting into Royal Banks
And arrows jetting upward to the moon,

Monogamy, St. Catherine Street, gold coin,
Classical Colleges and Bordeaux Gaol,

Asia and Europe by another route,
A Diênbiênphu around the globe.

And as I watched, the time for action struck.
The helpless actors moved to play their part.

A pistol went bang bang for Christ and France.
Another Indian died a Christian death.

That night red women wept white women's tears,
And white men snored like any Indian braves.

ODE TO CONFEDERATION
or HOW IT ALL HAPPENED

John Cabot was quick on the helm
And served a magnanimous Prince,
He discovered a wonderful realm
But it's been in a fog ever since.
We can't see the Smallwood for trees
And we know that this sea-faring folk
Would never have sunk to their knees
If they hadn't been utterly broke.

Newfoundland loses Dominion Status through bankruptcy and is pushed into Confederation.

The Scotsmen and Loyalists came
And took on a neck of the woods,
They carved out a tiny domain
And began to deliver the goods,
Till they fell for the plea to unite
In a flood of oration and wine;
They got their steam railway alright
But were left at the end of the line.

The Maritime Provinces are seduced by the blandishments of the Upper Canadians.

When Cartier raised up a flag
And planted a cross on the hill
He paid not a cent for the crag
Till history sent him the bill.
And when Maisonneuve slew the Chief
And the Indians grew Christian and poor,
Versailles heaved a sigh of relief
For the rule of the White Man was sure.

Jacques Cartier helps himself to Indian lands, and de Maisonneuve holds on to them.

St. Lawrence and Ottawa join
The jolly old jamboree,
Great Lakes in the groin
And profiteers out on a spree.
If you want to be righteous and rich
And to know you have God on your side
You won't find a cosier niche
Than Toronto can always provide.

Ontario piles gold-brick on gold-brick.

Saskatchewan leapt in the lead
By smiting capitalists' thighs.
The long-suffering farmers were freed
And rain blossomed down from the skies.
But next door a Sunday-school chump
Brought political pots to the boil.
And his province escaped from the slump
By the strikes of Imperial Oil.

The CCF comes to power in Saskatchewan while Aberhart sells Social Credit to Alberta.

Far west where the sun has to set
Lies a fabulous parcel of ground,
It hasn't made history yet
But they play golf there all the year round.
The wall of the Rockies is high
And we none of us go there too often
But Craigellachie means till we die
That they drove the last spike in our coffin.

British Columbia tops it off.

Here's a jug of the best,
Fill up a bowl for the soul,
There's a bumper crop in the West,
Oil is beginning to roll.
Pipe me my natural gas,
Dig me my atom-bomb ores,
Up with the Kicking Horse Pass,
And down with the Liberal bores!

Chorus

MARTINIGRAM

The key person in the whole business
I said raising my Martini damn that woman
she didn't look where she was going sorry
it won't stain the key person what? oh it's
you Georgina no I won't be there tomorrow
see you some day the key person in the whole
business is not the one oh hello James yes
we're having a wonderful time not the one you
love but it's no thank you no more just now
not the one you love but it's the one who
does the hell's bells there's a stone in my olive

THE BARTAIL COCK

Rounding a look
Her lightened tips
Tackled my fincy
So I gave her the um con.
She was right, all tight,
But clan, did she have mass!

Hatting her pair
She rossed off her tum
Barred at the leer-tender
Tumbled her way to my fable
And cholding my hair
Lissed me on the kips.

I skoated in the fly!

CARLOS CAT

(After a poem by William Carlos Williams)

As the cat
stepped into the
flowerpot
first the right forefoot
then the hind
the poem was
over

so CARLOS
wrote it down and
hearing the Brahms
variations on a
theme by Handel

I suddenly saw the cat
watching CARLOS
writing the poem at a
little desk so

I had to write this
poem about me
watching the cat
watching CARLOS and

that is already a
bigger poem and
possibly nothing more
should be written
on this
cat

PERIGOURDINE

Souls of poets yet to be
Feasts Elysian you may see
Finer than in Keats's fable
Spread on any Paris table.
Poularde Demi Deuil en Vessie
Tops the victory of Crécy.
From the simple English hen
L'Oeuf Mollet Parisienne
Never dropped. No taverns know
La Timbale de Ris de Veau.
And when you are born, compare
With your native country fare
Le Pigeon Cocotte Grand'mère.
Then consume a Coupe de Fruits
A L'Armagnac, Crème Chantilly,
Meringue Glacée, Crème Fraîche,
Le Canard Nantais aux Pêches,
Or a hundred other trifles
That a jolly poet rifles
From a menu by the Seine
While his tongue rolls round again.

These are dishes so divine
They invite the sister wine.
You may let your fancy vary
From a glass of mere Canary!
Clos des Cortons, Muscadet,
Pouilly-Fuissé and Vouvray,
Châteauneuf du Pape, Meurseault,
Mouton Cadet, Clos Vougeot,
With such other lovely loot
As Pol Roger, Cliquot brut,
Will bring a gleam to poet's eyes
And make them write upon the skies.

MY THREE DOCTORS

Doctor Body is the best –
Sends no bills and takes no rest.
Brings to pain and broken bone
Pharmacopoeia all his own.

His assistant, Dr. Bed,
Likes to coddle me instead.
Soothes me in my private room,
Recreates the healthy womb.

Meet the jolliest of the three,
My psychiatrist, Dr. B.
Dear old Bottle! Slaps my back
When I'm just about to crack.

I went to bat for the Lady Chatte
    Dressed in my bib and gown.
The judges three glared down at me
    The priests patrolled the town.

My right hand shook as I reached for that book
    And rose to play my part.
For out on the street were the marching feet
    Of the League of the Sacred Heart.

The word "obscene" was supposed to mean
    "Undue exploitation of sex."
This wording's fine for your needs and mine
    But it's far too free for Quebec's.

I tried my best, with unusual zest,
    To drive my argument through.
But I soon got stuck on what rhymes with "muck"
    And that dubious word "undue."

So I raised their sights to the Bill of Rights
    And cried: "Let freedom ring!"
Showed straight from the text that freedom of sex
    Was as clear as anything.

Then I plunged into love, the spell that it wove,
    And its attributes big and bold
Till the legal elect all stood erect
    As my rapturous tale was told.

The judges' sighs and rolling of eyes
    Gave hope that my case was won,
Yet Mellors and Connie still looked pretty funny
    Dancing about in the sun.

What hurt me was not that they did it a lot
  And even ran out in the rain,
'Twas those curious poses with harebells and roses
  And that dangling daisy-chain.

Then too the sales made in the paperback trade
  Served to aggravate judicial spleen,
For it seems a high price will make any book nice
  While its mass distribution's obscene.

Oh Letters and Law are found in the raw
  And found on the heights sublime,
But D.H. Lawrence would view with abhorrence
  This Jansenist pantomime.

SNOWBALLS FOR YOU, MR. JOSEPHS

("No doubt some scholarship assistance is valuable and stimulating, but once
started it has a way of snowballing." Mr. Devereux C. Josephs, President, New
York Life Insurance Company)

When the first Sputnik went up
Everyone cried "Education! Education!
This is what we need to beat the Russians!"
At last we had found a value in education.
So letters from parents flooded the newspapers,
Heads of colleges made great statements,
Businessmen said the academic year must be lengthened
As they saw the summer jobs declining,
Duplessis said education must remain provincial
(Little Laika, looking down from her moon,
Could easily see education was provincial)
Professors felt pleased they might soon be able to study
And still pay their food bills.
It was all very encouraging.

Then the Americans sent up the Explorer
And the shouting died down.

Governors shook their heads sadly
And raised university fees.
Duplessis refused to see the students.
Recession set in, no one having enough education
To know how to stop it.
The Conservatives were back.
This was no time for coddling the young.

"Students must learn to pay for what they get,"
Said Mr. Josephs of the New York Life.
"Why shouldn't they borrow some of the cost?
Let them start their lives in debt.
No doubt, no doubt at all
Some scholarships are stimulating
But once started
It can snowball."

"Ha ha," said the Russians,
 In their free universities.
"Bow wow," said little Laika.

FOR WHOM THE BELL TOLLS

For the twenty-sixth anniversary
Of the Battle of Britain
The official films
Replayed on television
Were sponsored by the Bell Telephone Company,
And Churchill's immortal words
Were interrupted
By Sunday's long-distance rates.

Seldom in the whole history
Of the mass media
Has so much had to be borne
By so many
For so few.

PRACTICAL MEN

"No health insurance for Canada"
   says the Chamber of Commerce
sitting in the Chateau Frontenac
   every member insured personally
against sickness, accident, fire, theft,
   and housemaids falling off step-ladders.

"It might lead to state medicine"
   warn these prophets
who have been educated in state schools
   and have mostly graduated
from state universities.

ARS MEDICA

If you ever thought I had a touch of the old Diogenes
Let me tell you, Sir, I have a great deal more than that – a dose of
  nothing less than Staphylococcus Pyogenes!
No, friends, this is neither funereal
Nor venereal,
But there is no graph that can shock us
So much as the life-curve of this staphylococcus.
It has reduced my medical advisers to the condition of pathetic
  neurotics
By the way it breeds new strains to evade their antibiotics.

One day I introduced my new staph to my old amoeba.
Boy! This was like the meeting of King Solomon and the Queen
  of Sheba,
From which there came offspring of such verve, sparkle and dash
That I immediately packed them off with my heartiest best
  wishes (collect) to Ogden Nash.

GIVE A PINT: SAVE A LIFE

The Red Cross worker
Took pints of blood
From 325 convicts
In Bordeaux Gaol.

Among them
A man condemned to death.

First you prick the finger
For the blood test,
Then you press the finger down
To stop the bleeding.
Then you take the address:
All blood donors
Must give their address.

But his fingernails were too long
To press down.
He had not been allowed any scissors
Lest he try to "cheat justice."

And the address?
"My address," he said,
"What's the use?"

What's the use!

NATIONAL IDENTITY

The Canadian Centenary Council
Meeting in le Reine Elizabeth hotel
To seek those symbols
Which will explain ourselves to ourselves
Evoke bi-cultural responses
And prove that something called Canada
Really exists in the hearts of all
Handed out to every delegate
At the start of proceedings
A portfolio of documents
On the cover of which appeared
In gold letters
        not
A Mari Usque Ad Mare
        not
Dieu Et Mon Droit
        not
E Pluribus Unum
        but
COURTESY OF COCA-COLA LIMITED

LINES WRITTEN DURING THE McGILL CONVOCATION
OCTOBER 6, 1966

Soon we'll come no more, my hearties,
To these classrooms and these courts,
Armed with righteousness and power
And command of leading sports.

For the flagpole flags are changing
And there comes another king
While the lion lies asleeping
And the wasps have lost their sting.

COUNTER-SIGNS

By moving west
I learned how to go east.
By standing on my head
I found out the importance of feet.
Through stumbling
I discovered dancing,
Through slaughter,
Kindness.
Wanting to go somewhere
I started in the other direction.
At last I know where I am.
I am nowhere at all.

FEED-BACK

I measured him.
I weighed him.
I timed him.
I tested his blood.
I put radioactive particles into him
and followed their movements.
I enclosed him in a sound-proof box
for three days
and checked his memory.
I took him to a topless tavern
and then to the Canadian Senate.
I made him eat muktuk.
I asked him whether he liked his father
better than his mother.

Looking at me wearily he said:
"How long will it take
before I'll know if I'm suitable?"
"Not long now," I answered,
"we'll soon have everything taped."

But just as I was feeding all the material
into the IBM computer
the poor fool dropped out
grew a beard
bought a guitar
and began writing songs.

CYCLES

Take these berries, the blood of flowers dead,
a season's calendar, a torn-off page
of the bush-year, one more to go when the leaves,
sucked dry, float down to make more ground
around the roots that feed the berry-flowers.

        a small boy rolls a hoop
          no parts of it escape
            the rise and fall and rise
              that give the hoop its shape
              the circle of its hope
              the circle of our days
                the down before the rise
                  the never settling down. . . .

X
Trouvailles:
Poems From Prose

THE INDIANS SPEAK AT EXPO '67

When the White Man came
We welcomed him
With love

We sheltered him
Fed him
Led him through the forest

The great explorers of Canada
Travelled in Indian canoes
Wore Indian snow-shoes
Ate Indian food
Lived in Indian houses

They could not have lived
Or moved
Without Indian friends

The early missionaries thought us Pagans
They imposed upon us their own stories
Of God
Of heaven and hell
Of sin and salvation

The White Men fought each other for our land
We were embroiled in the White Man's wars

The wars ended in treaties
And our lands
Passed into the White Man's hands

(From inscriptions found in different rooms at the Indians of Canada Pavilion,
EXPO '67.)

NOR'WESTERS

While the trade is confined
to a single company,
that company is bound
by every motive which self-interest can supply
to preserve the savages from
war,
drunkenness,
idleness
or whatever else
would divert them from the chase,
and lessen the quantity of skins
annually received
at the different posts.

(From "On the Origin and Progress of the North West Company," 1811, quoted in *McGillivray Lord of the Northwest*, by Marjorie Wilkins Campbell, p. 163.)

THE ROBINSON TREATIES

In consequence of the discovery
Of minerals,
On the shores of Lakes Huron and Superior,
The government of the late Province of Canada,
Deemed it desirable,
To extinguish
The Indian
Title,

And in order to that end,
In the year 1850,
Entrusted the duty
To the late Honourable William B. Robinson,
Who discharged his duties
With great tact and judgement,
Succeeding in making two treaties,
Which were the forerunners of the future treaties,
And shaped their course.

(From *The Treaties of Canada with the Indians of Manitoba*, by Alexander
Morris, Toronto, 1880, p. 16.)

THE BEAVER

The beaver
is a most respectable animal
but he is also a type
of unvarying instincts
and Old-World traditions.
He does not improve,
and becomes extinct
rather than change his ways.

(Sir William Dawson, 1863, quoted in *Saturday Night*, January 1967.)

TREATY

Ningaram ✱ ✱ ✱ ✱ (his mark)

We
The undersigned Chiefs and Warriors
On behalf of the people
Of the Newash Band
Of Chippewa Indians
Residing at Owen Sound
Send greeting.
Whereas we and our people
Having the fullest confidence
In the eternal care
And good intentions
Of our kind Father the Governor General
Towards all his Indian children
And foreseeing all the benefits
That we and our posterity
Are likely to derive
From the surrender of large portions
Of our Reserve
In the year of our Lord 1854,
We have after mature consideration
In several full councils
Held at our village of Newash
Arrived at the conclusion
That it will be to our advantage
To place at the disposal of our Father
The Governor General
The land upon which we now reside
Commonly known as the Newash
Or Owen Sound Reserve
In order that he may cause the same
To be sold for our benefit.

Wabuminguam ◎ ◎ ◎ ◎ (his mark)

(From a Treaty displayed at the Indians of Canada Pavilion, EXPO '67.)

VILLAINOUS DENS

The Toronto Leader of Saturday
Has the following:
A couple of cases
Of a sad and startling nature
Have just been brought under the notice
Of the Police Magistrate,
Which show that there are existing in this city
Villainous dens
Whose proprietors are in the habit
Of enticing
Unsuspecting girls
From the paths of virtue.

(From *The Gazette*, Montreal, February 13, 1867.)

THE ARCHBISHOP SPEAKS

Before Confederation had been decreed
By the Imperial Parliament,
And while the project
Was yet only a project,
It was doubtless permissible
To discuss it,
And even to employ all fair means
To prevent it becoming law.
Indeed many people,
Of whose patriotism there can be no question,
Thought they saw in it
Serious dangers for the future,
And took it to be their duty
To oppose it.
But, today,
Discussion is no longer possible;
The law is promulgated;
The work of authority should be respected;
To refuse submission to it
Would be to overset the established order of God,
and to resist His will;
It would be to tend toward anarchy, treason, revolt,
And all the evils in their train.

(From a pastoral letter issued by the Roman Catholic Archbishop of Quebec,
Mgr. de Tloa, on the subject of Confederation. *The Gazette*, Montreal,
June 18, 1867.)

I propose
The adoption of the rainbow
As our emblem.
By the endless variety of its tints
The rainbow will give an excellent idea
Of the diversity of races, religions, sentiments and interests
Of the different parts
Of the Confederation.
By its slender and elongated form
The rainbow would afford
A perfect representation
Of the geographical configuration
Of the Confederation.
By its lack of consistence –
An image without substance –
The rainbow would represent aptly
The solidity of our Confederation.
An emblem we must have,
For every great empire has one;
Let us adopt
The rainbow.

(Henri Joly de Lotbinière, quoted in F.H. Underhill, *In Search of Canadian Liberalism*, Toronto, 1960.)

OTTAWA BECOMES CIVILIZED

Ottawa is becoming somewhat civilized.
Private parties are numerous;
The band of the 100th plays in public
Occasionally;
There has been a concert or two;
The Civil Service Regiment has established
A mess
Of its own
And there is promised a masquerade
At the rink
In a day or two.
Let us exclaim with Audley:
"The gods give us joy."

(From *The Gazette*, Montreal, January 23, 1867.)

Court Circular

GOVERNMENT HOUSE —
His Excellency the Governor-
General presented the Gov-
ernor-General's cup and the
Lady Tweedsmuir Cup to the
winners of the Governor-
General's competition at Gov-
ernment House on Friday.
Their excellencies afterwards
gave a reception for members
of the Governor-General's
Curling Club and for mem-
bers of clubs competing for
the Governor-General's Cup
and the Lady Tweedsmuir
Cup.

COURT CIRCULAR

Government House

His Excellency the Governor General
Presented the Governor General's Cup
And
The Lady Tweedsmuir Cup
To the winners of the Governor General's competition
At
Government House
On Friday.

Their Excellencies afterwards
Gave a reception
For members of the Governor General's Curling Club
And
For members of clubs competing
For the Governor General's Cup
And
The Lady Tweedsmuir Cup.

(*The Montreal Star*, July 15, 1965.)

USHERING IN THE QUIET REVOLUTION

J.- OMER DIONNE
Candidat pour le comté de COMPTON
(complete description)

Agriculteur, 55 ans,
10 enfants.
Membre de la Ligue du Sacré-Coeur.
Une soeur religieuse,
Supérieure d'un hôpital au Nouveau-Brunswick;
Deux cousins missionaires,
Son neveu est curé
De St. Alcide.

Frédéric COITEUX
Candidat pour l'Assomption
(complete description)

Cultivateur, 58 ans,
10 enfants,
Vice-prés. de l'Office
Des Marchés des Tabacs du Québec.
Membre de la Ligue du Sacré-Coeur
Et marguillier.
Un fils, clerc de St. Viateur,
Une fille religieuse au Mont-Jésus-Marie,
Une fille Oblate de Marie-Immaculée.

(From the Quebec Liberal Party Campaign pamphlet giving the qualifications of
its candidates for the election of 1960.)

AIRDROP, CAPE DORSET, CHRISTMAS 1964

I wish you could have seen
The airdrop.

Although only two parachutes came down
All the excitement
Of awaiting their arrival
Was there.

The airplane
A big Hercules
Flew low over the settlement.
It was dark
And we could only see
The flashing red lights.

Then in the sky
Two little lights
Moving slowly down
And above them
Opening like giant flowers
The huge 'chutes.
In the dark
Everyone began to clap hands
And shout.

The first plane arrived
Just before Christmas
And with it came
As well as letters and cards
Three months' copies
Of the *Ottawa Journal*!

(From a private letter dated January 24, 1965.)

BRITISH INDUSTRIALIST APPROVES APARTHEID

is the headline. Sir Francis de Guingand
Chairman of Rothman's of Pall Mall, Ltd.,
(substantial cigarette and tobacco holdings in South Africa)
said black Africans in general
are "just too immature for self-government."
While admitting
"It's an immensely complex problem, of course,"
he said he was "all in favour of separate development."
Apparently the Portuguese colonies
are doing "awfully well, you know,"
while black Africans
"are killing each other."
"Those Somali chaps –
they're bound to cause trouble.
Same thing in the Congo.
Awful mess.
And Burundi,
Urundi,
or whatever you call the place.
Killing each other by the thousands.
Dreadful,
just dreadful."
And as for Nyerere of Tanzania,
he is "playing far too much
into the hands
of the wretched Chinese."

(From *The Gazette*, Montreal, October 10, 1966.)

ONE CURE FOR LONELINESS

Noted
the recent letters
from people who are lonely
and find time hanging heavily
on their hands.

Some form of hobby
can serve to interest
such folk.
Such a hobby need not be expensive
nor demand undue space
or equipment.

News events
or stories and articles
from the press and magazines
can be clipped and pasted
in a scrapbook.

This book could be
I am told
as cheap as a five-cent copy book
and a jar of paste
is mentioned
at about
nineteen cents.

(*The Montreal Star*, July 15, 1965.)

LA PLANIFICATION FAMILIALE AU QUÉBEC

L'intérêt qu'on porte à la contraception
est relativement
récent. Aussi,
une foule d'aspects
de ce domaine complexe
n'ont pas encore été
suffisamment étudiés.
Nombre de chercheurs travaillent
à l'amélioration
des techniques contraceptives,
mais on se préoccupe trop peu
des conséquences
d'une utilisation accrue
de ces techniques
de plus en plus efficaces.
Notre population n'est elle pas menacée
d'extinction!
Qu'arrive-t-il au couple
qui s'était accommodé
de méthodes non efficaces
ou très restrictives!
N'y a-t-il pas danger de
déséquilibre!

L'Association pour la planification familiale
de Montréal
organise un forum
sur le sujet.

Le forum se tiendra
le 6 Octobre 1966
au Monastère
St-Albert le Grand.

L'entrée est gratuite.

(From a circular distributed by The Planned Family Association.)

THE CANADIAN SOCIAL REGISTER

(A Social Register for Canada was promoted in Montreal in 1947. On the
Advisory Committee were names like Rt. Hon. Louis St. Laurent, Sir Ellsworth
Flavelle, Air Marshal Bishop, Rear-Admiral Brodeur, Hon. J. Earl Lawson,
Hartland Molson, and others. A Secret Committee was to screen all applicants.
All quotations in this poem are taken verbatim from the invitation sent out to
prospective members.)

Reader, we have the honour to invite you to become a "Member
    of the Social Register,"
For the paltry fee of $125 per annum.
This "work of art, done in good taste," and listing annually the
    "Notables of the Dominion,"
Will contain nothing but "Ladies and Gentlemen pre-eminent in
    the Higher Spheres,"
A list, indeed, of "First Families,"
Who are "the very fabric of our country."
Thus shall we "build up in the Nation's First Families
A consciousness of their role in the life of a civilized democracy."
Thus shall we bring "added dignity and profound significance
To our cultural way of life."
Through deplorable lack of vision, in times past,
Men who were "great Canadians, have everlastingly passed into
    oblivion,"
Leaving no "footprints on the sands of time."
Somehow, despite their pre-eminence, they have disappeared.
Shall we, through "tragic shortsightedness," let the leaders of this era
"Disappear into the realm of eternal silence?"
"Shall there be no names, no achievements, to hearten and
    strengthen on-coming generations in time of stress?"
If they have failed to make history, shall they fail to make The
    Canadian Social Register?
No – not if they can pay $125 annually,
And pass our Secret Committee.
For there is a "Secret Committee of seven members,"
Who will "determine the eligibility of those applying for
    membership."
Thus will the Social Register be "accepted in the most fastidious
    circles."

And to aid the Secret Committee you will send
The name of your father and the maiden name of your mother,
And the address of your "summer residence,"
(For of course you have a summer residence).
You may also submit, with a glossy print of yourself,
"Short quotations from laudatory comments received on diverse
        public occasions."
When printed, the Register will be sent,
Free, gratis, and not even asked for,
To (among many others) the "King of Sweden," the "President of
        Guatemala," and the "Turkish Public Library."

Reader, this will be "a perennial reminder"
Of the people (or such of them as pass the Secret Committee)
Who "fashioned this Canada of ours,"
For "One does not live only for toil and gain,"
Not, anyway, in First Families. It is comforting to believe
That while we "walk the earth," and pay $125,
And "after we have passed on," there will remain
"In the literature of the Universe," and particularly in the
        "Turkish Public Library,"
This "de luxe edition," "these unique and dignified annals,"
"These priceless and undying memories," with laudatory
        comments chosen by ourselves,
To which "succeeding First Families and historians alike will look,"
For "knowledge, guidance and inspiration."
Lives rich in eligibility will be "written large,"
(But within "a maximum of one thousand words")
"For all men to see and judge."
The "glorious dead," too,
These "selfless and noble defenders of Canada's honour,"
Will be incorporated in the Social Register
"Without any financial remuneration,"
Assuming, of course, that they are all
"Sons and daughters of its Members."

Reader, as you may guess, the Register
Was not "a spur of the moment idea."
It was "long and carefully nurtured,"

And "counsel was sought in high and authoritative places,"
So that it may "lay a basis upon which prominent Canadians will
    henceforth be appraised
As they go striding down the years,"
Paying their $125,
And receiving a "world-wide, gratuitous distribution,"
Even unto "the Turkish Public Library."

"Si monumentum requiris, circumspice!"
On this note, we both end.

(From *The Gazette*, Montreal, February 25, 1967, reporting a finding of the
Carter Royal Commission on Taxation.)

CENT ANS D'INJUSTICE

Low income individuals
and families
pay a higher proportion
of their incomes
in all kinds of taxes
than those
with higher incomes.

DEW LINES 1956

Beards dip in coldest dew
Bedabbled with the dew
Bright dew is shaking
DISTANT EARLY WARNING

Honey-headed dew of slumber
Dew of summer nights collected
Dew shall weep thy fall tonight
DISTANT EARLY WARNING

Dew that on the violet lies
Whose wine was the bright dew
Dew will rust them
DISTANT EARLY WARNING

Falls the dew on the face of the dead
On whom the dew of heaven drops?
Who hath begotten the drops of dew?
DISTANT EARLY WARNING

There rain'd a ghastly dew
With anguish moist and fever dew
Red dew of Olivet
DISTANT EARLY WARNING

(Oxford *Dictionary of Quotations*, verbal "Dew.")

XI
Translations

SONNET IN DIALOGUE ON THE NATURE OF LOVE

(Serafino Dall'Aquila, 1446-1500)

When is thy birthday, Love? – When earth regains
Her brightest flowers and loveliest attire. –
Of what art thou begotten? – Of the fire
That every wanton prisons in his veins. –
How then hast caused in me these bitter pains? –
By chills of fear, and burning of desire. –
Where dwell'st thou first? – In warm hearts, that inspire
My swift embrace, and soon accept my chains. —
Say now who nursed thee? — Youth, and those who go
To seek adventure at his court alway:
Beauty, Conceit, Pomp, Braggadocio. —
Art nourished? – Yes, on looks that dart and play. –
Can neither age nor death destroy thee? – No:
I am reborn a thousand times each day.

EPIGRAM

(Giovanni Gherardo De' Rossi, 1754-1827)

Love would heap scorn upon her sister spring
For the brief stay and hasty sojourning
    Of her stray flowers.
But that fair season answered, "Oh, then those,
    Your amorous hours,
Outlast, perhaps, the blooming of my rose?"

FAREWELL TO THE FRENCHMEN RETURNING FROM NEW FRANCE TO GALLIC FRANCE, 25 AUGUST 1606

(*Marc Lescarbot*, 1570-1640?)

(This farewell was addressed to the members of Poutrincourt's second expedition to Port Royal ((now Annapolis Royal, Nova Scotia)) who were returning to France leaving Lescarbot behind to winter in the little settlement on the Bay of Fundy. It is almost certainly the first poem written in America north of the Spanish frontier. It was revised and published in Paris in the author's *Les Muses de la Nouvelle France*, 1609. This translation is from the first version as it stands in the Biencourt-Harvard pamphlet, supplied to me by Peter Dale Scott. A reprint of the poem is included in the Champlain Society's translation of Lescarbot's *Histoire de la Nouvelle France*, Vol. 3, Toronto, 1914.)

Go then, set sail, O goodly company
Whose noble hearts withstood courageously
The dreadful fury of both wind and wave
The cruel blows the many seasons gave
To plant among us France's glorious name
And 'mid such hazards to preserve her fame.
Go then, set sail, and soon may each attain
The home fires of his Ithaca again;
And may we also, yet another year
See this whole company returning here.

Worn with fatigue you leave us, and we share
With you an equal weight of mutual care;
You, that no dread diseases bring their doles
To make to Pluto offering of our souls:
We, that no fitful wave or hidden rock
Strike your frail craft with unexpected shock.
But here resemblance fails, the likeness ends,
'Tis you who go to see congenial friends
In language, habits, customs and religion
And all the lovely scenes of your own nation,
While we among the savages are lost
And dwell bewildered on this clammy coast
Deprived of due content and pleasures bright
Which you at once enjoy when France you sight.

But what I say is wrong! In this lone land
All his soul needs the just man may command
And will God's power and graciousness revere
If he will contemplate the beauty here.
For should one travel all the earth around
And test the worth of every plot of ground
No place so fair, so perfect will he find
That our Port Royal will not leave far behind.
Perhaps you would on open country gaze?
These sloping banks are washed by numerous bays.
One hundred hills as well would please your eye?
Below one hundred all these waters lie.
Do you then seek the pleasure of the chase?
On every side great forests it embrace.
Are gamey birds desired for your meat?
Each season does its ordered flocks repeat.
Have you a longing for a varied dish?
The bounteous sea will gratify each wish.
Love you the gentle prattling of the rills?
They flow profusely from th'enlacing hills.
Would you enjoy the sight of islands green?
Two city-size within this port are seen.
Do you admire loquacious Echo's rhymes?
Here Echo can reply full thirty times,
For when the cannon's thunder outward sounds
Full thirty times the reverberant boom rebounds
As loud as if Megaera furious sought
To bring this mighty universe to nought.
Would you survey deep rivers in their course?
Three here pay tribute with their wavy force,
Of which the Eel* that sweeps the most terrain,
Bears down the proudest billow to the main,
And almost deafens with her boisterous pace
Not the Catadupois,** but this wild race.
Would you, in brief, your enemies withstand?
No fear is here save from heaven's wrathful hand,
For with two bulwarks nature fortified
Our entrance road so well, the countryside
From every threat kept safe, can rest in peace
And season after season live at ease.

Corn still is lacking, and no grapes are found
To make thy name through all the world renowned,
But should Almighty God our labours bless
Thou soon shalt feel celestial plenteousness
Pour down upon thee like the early dew
That, softly falling, doth parch'd earth renew
In midsummer. And though we do not wrest
The richness of the gold mine from thy breast,
Bronze, silver, iron, that thy thickset woods
Guard as in trust, these too are richest goods
For a beginning; someday may be found
The gold that waits its turn beneath the ground.
But now we are content thou may'st supply
Both corn and wine, then afterward may'st try
A more ambitious flight (the grass that girds
Thy waters could supply a thousand herds)
And build the cities, strongholds, settlements,
To give retreat to pioneers from France
And bring conversion to this savage nation
That has no God, no laws and no religion.

O thrice Almighty God whom I adore,
Whose sun upon this countryside doth pour
His dawn, I pray Thee, do not longer wait,
Have pity on this people's poor estate,
Who languish, hoping Thy more perfect light
Too long, alas! withholden from their sight.

Dupont, whose name is graven on the sky
For having stood with matchless bravery
Against a thousand ills, a thousand pains,
Enough to crush the spirit in your veins,
When you were left here with the governance
Of those, who in this country of New France
Sustained with ardour equal to your own
The long and bitter absence from their home —
As soon as you shall come to greet your King
Remind him of those days of crusading
When his forefathers fought to Palestine
For love of Christian law, and held the line

'Gainst furious Saracen and all his host
Offering their lives along the Memphis coast
To whim of wind and wave in that dread land,
To dripping scimitar in sudden hand;
Tell him that here with little cost or blood
With which strong arms can taint the murderous sword
He may surround himself with equal glory
And add a greater grandeur to his story.

Go then, set forth, O Frenchmen of stout heart,
While now our sails are calling us to start
Toward the Armouchiquois, past Malebarre,
To find another port to serve as bar
To threatening foe, or as a post to extend
A sheltered welcome to the incoming friend
And there discover if New France's soil
Will justify our faith-inspired toil.

Neptune, if e'er thou hast thy favour cast
On those whose lives upon thy waves are passed,
Good Neptune, grant us what we most desire,
Safe berth in friendly port, so thine Empire
May thereupon be known in countless regions
And soon be visited by all the nations.

(*The Eel River: now the Annapolis River.)
(**Catadupois: people living beside one of the Nile's cataracts.)

TO MADAME DU CHÂTELET

(François-Marie de Voltaire, 1694-1778)

If you would have my love reborn
Give back to me my youthful ways,
And mingle with my twilight days
The zest and eagerness of morn.

From pleasant groves where Bacchus bold
With Venus panders to desire
Time grasps my hand with firmer hold
And warns me that I must retire.

From his unalterable rule
Let us, at least, find some relief.
None are so doomed to every grief
As greybeards who still play the fool.

Let us forswear, when youth is done,
The transports of the amorous breast.
We live but two brief spans at best;
Let wisdom be in charge of one.

What? Are the days then gone, when rife
Were tenderness, enchantment, love,
Those consolations from above
For all the bitterness of life?

Yes, twice to death are mortals brought:
We cease to love, and to endear.
This one's a death most hard to bear,
But to stop living — that is nought.

Therefore I grieved when I was past
The errors of my youthful days,
And long my heart, still half ablaze,
Regretted joys that could not last.

Till down from regions undefiled
Sweet Friendship hastened to my aid.
She was no less a tender maid
Than love, although less warm and wild.

So, drawn by beauty in her eyes
And by her novel grace, I keep
Her constant suitor; but I weep
That she alone can be my prize.

CRITIQUE OF POETRY

(Paul Eluard, 1895-1952)

It is well-known that I hate the power of the bourgeois
And the power of the cops and priests
But I hate even more the man who does not hate it
As I do
With all his might.

I spit in the face of the man who is smaller than life
Who of all my poems does not prefer this *Critique of Poetry*.

WARNING

(*Paul Eluard*)

The night before his death
Was the shortest in his life
The idea that he still existed
Burned the blood in his wrists
The weight of his body terrified him
His strength made him groan
It was from this depth of horror
That he began to smile
He did not have ONE comrade
He had millions and millions
To avenge him as he knew well
And the daybreak dawned for him.

TRUE JUSTICE

(Paul Eluard)

It is the generous law of man
From grapes to fashion wine
From coal to fashion fire
From kisses to fashion men

It's the hard law of man
To keep himself unscathed
In spite of wars and distress
In spite of the danger of death

It's the kindly law of man
To change water to light
The dream to reality
Enemies into brothers

Both an old and a new law
Which grows ever more true
From its source in the heart of a child
Up to its ultimate proof

THE FORERUNNER

(Jean-Charles Harvey, 1891-1967)

His probing thought cut lanes through custom and cant.
Always he followed the line of his farthest flight.
So they rose in a rage and tied his hands to his side.

His step was daring and sure on the tricky ground,
Marking a path where they said disaster lay.
So they bound his feet lest he show that the road was clear.

With sharper need he spoke to the captive world
And lit with signal words the slope of escape.
So they stopped his mouth lest he waken the multitude.

His glance still burned with the hungry flame of his mind.
None who walked in that light went blind as before.
So they sealed his eyes to prove their power and ease.

Then fearing the strength and hope in his living name
They cried for his blood and washed their hands as he died.
But swift from his grave the heirs of his struggle rose.

THE PHILANTHROPISTS

(Jean Narrache, 1893-1970)

It's one of the sports of millionaires
And swell fun for the well-heeled guys
T'think up new ways of fixin' affairs
So's to steal all the limelight money buys.

They'll give handouts to hospitals anyday,
Welfare Societies and homes for the sick. . . .
But it's all clipped off of our pay
At fleecing us they're too damn quick.

Newspapers build 'em up as philanthropists;
They're the big shots! They're sitting pretty!
But not a red cent really comes from their fists,
'Cause we're the poor dopes that sweeten their kitty.

Others who open nurseries and put statues up
Give Stations of the Cross and bells for churches
For their needy parents haven't a loaf or a cup,
Yet they're treated by all as though they were saints on perches.

And some who're nothing but pious deceivers
Screw their workers till they're ready to drop,
And then to attract all the true believers
Get a fat priest to come and bless their shop.

All the time he was preachin' around
Our Lord used to say: "Don't profess
So's to have all your good deeds crowned;
What your right hand's doin' your left shouldn't guess."

There's a helluva big change since th' Apostles' days;
Now they give with the right hand while the other
Keeps diggin' into our pockets in a hundred ways;
And this is how man now "comforts" his brother.

(Original poem first published 1932.)

BIRD CAGE

(St.-Denys Garneau, 1912-1943)

I am a bird cage
A cage of bone
With a bird

The bird in the cage of bone
Is death building his nest

When nothing is happening
One can hear him ruffle his wings

And when one has laughed a lot
If one suddenly stops
One hears him cooing
Far down
Like a small bell

It is a bird held captive
This death in my cage of bone

Would he not like to fly away
Is it you who will hold him back
Is it I
What is it

He cannot fly away
Until he has eaten all
My heart
The source of blood
With my life inside

He will have my soul in his beak.

ACCOMPANIMENT

(St.-Denys Garneau)

I walk beside a joy
Beside a joy that is not mine
A joy of mine which I cannot share

I walk beside myself in joy
I hear my joyful footsteps walking beside me
But I cannot change places on the sidewalk
I cannot put my feet in those steps and say
        Look it is I

For the moment I am content with this company
But secretly I plot an exchange
By all sorts of devices, by alchemies,
By blood transfusions
Displacement of atoms
        by balancing tricks

So that one day, transposed,
I may be carried along by the dance of those steps of joy
With the sound of my own footsteps dying away beside me
With the fall of my own lost step
        fading to my left
Under the feet of a stranger
        who turns down a side street.

MY EYES A RIVER

(St.-Denys Garneau)

O my eyes this morning wide as rivers
O rivers of my eyes ready to reflect everything
And this freshness under my lids
Miraculous
Surrounding the images I see

As a stream refreshes an island
And as the flowing water encircles
The bathing girl, sun-drenched.

A DEAD MAN ASKS FOR A DRINK

(St.-Denys Garneau)

A dead man asks for a drink
The well no longer has as much water as we thought
Who will tell this to the dead man
The spring says my flow is not for him.

So look now all his maids are running off
Each with a bowl, for each her fountain-head
To slake the thirst of the master,
A dead man who asks for a drink.

This one collects in the depth of the nocturnal garden
The delicate pollen which seeps up from flowers
In the warmth which lingers as night closes in
She displays this flesh in front of him.

But the dead man still is thirsty and asks for a drink.

That one collects by the silver of moonlit meadows
The corollas that were closed by the coolness of evening
She fashions them into a well-rounded bouquet
A tender burden cool on the lips
And hurries to offer it to the master.

But the dead man is thirsty and asks for a drink.

Then the third and first of the three sisters
Hurries also into the fields
While there rises in the eastern sky
The bright menace of dawn.
She gathers into the net of her golden apron
Shining drops of morning dew
Fills a cup and offers it to the master.

But still he is thirsty and asks for a drink.

Then morning breaks in its glory
And spreads the light like a breeze through the valley
And the dead man ground to dust
The dead man pierced by rays like a mist
Dissolves and dies
And even his memory has vanished from the earth.

SPECTACLE OF THE DANCE

(St.-Denys Garneau)

My children you dance badly
One must admit it is difficult to dance here
In this lack of air
Here without that space which is the whole of the dance.

You do not know how to play with space
How to play in it
Without chains
Poor children who cannot play.

How can you hope to dance   I have seen the walls
The city cut off your vision at the start
Cut off at the shoulder your maimed vision
Before even one rhythmic movement
Before its outward reach and faraway resting
Its blossoming faraway beyond the landscape
Before the flowering of your vision   the blending with the sky
The marriage to the sky of the vision
A meeting of infinites   a clash
Of wonders

The dance is a second measure and a second departure
It takes possession of the world
After the first victory
Of the vision

Which itself leaves no mark on space
— Less even than the bird and its furrow
Even than song and its invisible passage
An imperceptible trembling of the air —
Which is an embrace through the immaterial
Nearest to the changeless transparency
As in a landscape there is a reflection on water
Which no one saw fall in the river.

For the dance is a paraphrase of the vision
The rediscovery of the road the eyes had lost in their search
A statelier pace slowing to recapture
From its source an enveloping enchantment.

AT ONE TIME

(St.-Denys Garneau)

At one time I made poems
That contained the whole light-ray
From the centre to the periphery and beyond
As if there was no periphery
                but the centre alone
And as if I were the sun: all around
                        limitless space
How one gathers impetus
                by flashing along this ray
How one develops the prodigious speed of a meteor
What central pull can then stop us from escaping
What dome in the hollow firmament from our piercing it
When one has this impetus to burst into the Au delà

But one learns that the earth is not flat
But a sphere and that the centre is not in the middle
But in the centre
And one learns the length of the ray
                this road too often travelled
And one soon knows about the surface of the globe
All measured inspected surveyed, an old trail
Trodden down

Then the frustrating task
Of pushing the perimeter to its limit
In the hope of a crack on the surface of the globe
In the hope of a bursting of the boundaries
Through which to reach freely again to air and to light

Alas, so soon despair,
The impetus of the whole light-ray becomes
This dead point on the surface

So a man
On too short a road, through fear of its destination,
Shortens his stride and delays his arrival
I have to become subtle

In order, by infinitely dividing the tiny distance
From the string to the bow,
To create through ingeniousness a space like the Beyond
And to find in this refuge the nourishment
For my life and my art.

PERPETUAL BEGINNING

(St.-Denys Garneau)

A man of uncertain age
Rather young and rather old
Looking quite inattentive
And with colourless glasses
Sits at the foot of a wall
At the foot of a wall facing a wall

He says I'm going to count from one to a hundred
At one hundred it will be finished
Finally once and for all
I begin, one, two and the rest....

But at seventy-three he's not too sure any more

It is like believing you're counting the strokes of midnight
                                and reaching eleven
It is so dark how can you know?
You try to recapture the rhythm from the intervals
But when did it all begin?

And you wait for the next hour

He says come on we've got to end this
Let's begin all over again
Once and for all
From one to a hundred
One....

WEIGHTS AND MEASURES

(St.-Denys Garneau)

It's not a question of pulling things along by the hair
Of tying a woman by the hair to the tail of a horse
Of lining up the dead one after the other
Along the sword's edge, the edge of time.

One can have fun tying knots in parallel lines
It's quite a metaphysical entertainment
Absurdity not being reduced to living with the nose of Cyrano
But looking at all this with head upside down
One catches glimmerings of other worlds
One sees cracks in our world which make holes

One can get angry at seeing holes in our world
One can be scandalized by a torn stocking or waistcoat
   a torn glove that shows the finger
One can insist that it all be patched up

But a hole in our world is something more important
Provided one catches one's feet in it and that one drops
    the head in
And that one drops oneself in headfirst
This lets us wander about and even return again
This allows us to measure the world on foot
    foot by foot.

THE GAME

(St.-Denys Garneau)

Don't bother me I'm terribly busy

A child is starting to build a village
It's a city, a county
And who knows
        Soon the universe.

He's playing

These wooden blocks are houses he moves about and castles
This board indicates a sloping roof
                not at all bad to look at
It's no small thing to know the place where the road of cards
                will turn
This could change completely
                the course of the river
Because of the bridge which makes so beautiful a reflection
          on the water of the carpet
It's easy to have a tall tree
And to put a mountain underneath
                so it'll be high up

Joy of playing! Paradise of invention!
But above all don't put your foot in the room
One never knows what might be in this corner
Or whether you are not going to crush the favourite
            among the invisible flowers

Here is my box of toys
Full of words for weaving marvellous patterns
For uniting separating matching
Now the unfolding of the dance
And soon a clear burst of the laughter
That you thought had been lost

A gentle flip of the finger
And the star
Which hung carelessly
At the end of too flimsy a thread of light
Falls and makes rings in the water

Of love and tenderness who would dare to doubt
But not two cents of respect for the established order
Or for politeness and this precious discipline
A levity and practices fit to scandalize grown-up people

He arranges words for you as if they were simple songs
And in his eyes one can read his mischievous pleasure
At knowing that under the words he moves everything about
And plays with the mountains
As if they were his very own.
He turns the room upside down and truly we've lost our way
As if it was fun just to fool people.

And yet in his left eye when the right is laughing
A supernatural importance is imparted to the leaf of a tree
As if this could be of great significance
Had as much weight in his scales
As the war of Ethiopia
In England's.

We are not bookkeepers

Everyone can see a green dollar bill
But who can see through it
                    except a child
Who like him can see through it with full freedom
Without being in the least bothered by it
                    or its limitations
Or by its value of exactly one dollar

For he sees through this window thousands of marvellous toys
And has no wish to choose between these treasures
Neither desire nor necessity
Not he
For his eyes are wide open to take everything.

THE LEAN GIRL

(Anne Hébert, 1916-)

I am a lean girl
And I have beautiful bones.

I tend them with great care
And feel strange pity for them.

I continually polish them
As though they were old metal.

Now jewels and flowers
Are out of season.

One day I shall clasp my lover
And make of him a silver shrine.

I shall put myself
In the place of his absent heart.

O well-filled recess,
Who is this cold guest suddenly in you?

You walk,
You move;
Each one of your gestures
Adorns with fear the enclosed death.

I take your trembling
As a gift.

And sometimes
Fastened in your breast,
I half open
My liquid eyes

And strange and childish dreams
Swirl
Like green water.

AS IF FOR A HOLIDAY

(Anne Hébert)

Down pours the sun
Down pours the sun
The earth is fulfilled
The garden is round.

I have lighted
Two candles,
Two wax fires
Like two yellow flowers.

Daylight destroys
The fires of night,
Two faded flowers
On the white stalks of the church.

The world conforms
The dead below
The live above.

The dead visit me
The world conforms
The dead below
The live above.

The dead bore me,
The live kill me.

I have lighted
Two trembling flowers,
I have taken my eyes
In my hands
Like pebbles of water

And I have danced
Idiot steps
Around my tears
As if for a holiday.

THE CLOSED ROOM

(*Anne Hébert*)

Who then brought me here?
There was certainly someone
Who prompted my steps.
But when did that happen?
With the connivance of what quiet friend?
The deep approval of what long night?

Who was it laid out the room?
In what calm moment
Was the low ceiling thought of
The small green table and the tiny knife
The bed of black wood
And all the glow of the fire
With its purple billowing skirts
Around its heart, held fast and secure,
Under the orange and blue flames?

Who then took the true measure
Of the trembling cross of my outstretched arms?
The four cardinal points
Start at my fingertips
Provided I turn myself round
Four times
For as long as will last the memory
Of day and of night.

When my heart was placed on the table
Who then laid the cover so carefully
Sharpened the little knife
Without any anxiety
Or hurry?

My flesh is bewildered and wastes away
Without this familiar guest
Torn from between its ribs.
The bright colour of blood
Seals the hollow vault

And my hands folded
Over this devastation
Grow cold and fascinated with emptiness.

O gentle body asleep
The bed of black wood enfolds you
And holds you tightly so long as you do not move.
Above all do not open your eyes!
Be very careful
If you are going to see
The gleaming table and the dishes spread!

Leave, leave the fire to colour
The room with its reflections,
And replenish your heart and your flesh;
Unhappy pair now separate and lost.

MANOR LIFE

(Anne Hébert)

Here is an ancestral manor
Without a table or fire
Or dust or carpets.

The perverse enchantment of these rooms
Lies wholly in their polished mirrors.

The only possible thing to do here
Is to look at oneself all day and all night.

Cast your image upon these brittle fountains
Your brittler image without shadow or colour.

See, these mirrors are deep
Like cupboards
There is always someone dead behind the quicksilver
Who soon covers your reflection
And clings to you like seaweed

Shapes himself to you, naked and thin,
And imitates love in a slow, bitter shiver.

THERE IS CERTAINLY SOMEONE

(Anne Hébert)

There is certainly someone
Who once killed me
And then walked away
On the tip of his toes
Without interrupting his perfect dance.

Who forgot to take me to bed
And left me standing
All tightly bound
On the road
My heart sealed up as before
My two eyes like
Their own pure image of water.

Who forgot to erase the beauty of the world
Around me
Forgot to close my hungry eyes
And permitted their wasted passion.

THE TWO HANDS

(Anne Hébert)

These two hands that we have,
The right closed
Or open;

The left open
Or closed.

And the two
Not waiting
For each other.

Two hands that are not joined,
Two hands that cannot join.

The one that we give
And the one that we keep;

The one that we know
And the other, the unknown.

This child's hand,
This woman's hand,
And sometimes this working hand,
Simple as the hand of a man.

Then this makes three!
And I discover
In myself
An infinite number
Of hands that reach
Toward me,
Like strangers
Of whom one is afraid.

O! who will give back to me
My two hands as one?
And the shore
That we touch
With both hands,
Working together,
Having discarded on the way
All these useless hands.

THE TOMB OF THE KINGS

(Anne Hébert)

I carry my heart on my fist
Like a blind falcon.

The taciturn bird gripping my fingers
A swollen lamp of wine and blood
I go down
Toward the tombs of the kings
Astonished
Scarcely born.

What Ariadne-thread leads me
Along the muted labyrinths?
The echo of my steps fades away as they fall.

(In what dream
Was this child tied by her ankle
Like a fascinated slave?)

The maker of the dream
Pulls on the cord
And my naked footsteps come
One by one
Like the first drops of rain
At the bottom of a well.

Already the odour stirs in swollen storms
Seeps under the edges of the doors
Of chambers secret and round
Where the folding beds are laid out.

The motionless desire of the sculptured dead lures me.
I behold with astonishment
Encrusted upon black bones
The blue stones gleaming.

A few tragedies patiently wrought
Lying on the breast of sleeping kings
As if they were jewels
Are offered me
Without tears or regrets.

In single rank arrayed:
The smoke of incense, the cake of dried rice,
And my trembling flesh:
A ceremonial and submissive offering.

A gold mask on my absent face
Violet flowers for eyes,
The shadow of love paints me in small sharp strokes,
And this bird I have breathes
And complains strangely.

A long tremor
Like a wind sweeping from tree to tree,
Shakes the seven tall ebony Pharaohs
In their stately and ornate cases.

It is only the profundity of death which persists,
Simulating the ultimate torment
Seeking its appeasement
And its eternity
In a faint tinkle of bracelets
Vain rings, alien games
Around the sacrificed flesh.

Greedy for the fraternal source of evil in me
They lay me down and drink me;
Seven times I know the tight grip of the bones
And the dry hand that seeks my heart to break it.

Livid and satiated with the horrible dream
My limbs freed
And the dead thrust away from me, assassinated,
What glimmer of dawn strays in here?
What then makes this bird quiver
And turn toward morning
Its blinded eyes?

BLIND SEASON

(*Anne Hébert*)

For a long time we have kept the olden days at liberty in
the back rooms

Have left them free to roam all over the house, entrusted them to time
and put them to work again like dreams

They have paraded from room to room, each figure captured
again one by one in the row of mirrors

Have worn themselves out, have withered from the living-room
to the front porch where the golden rays of morning break
through the open door

Summer came shot with rays, the mother image lay down to die

Memories turn around at the violet centre of the too blue
places and our hearts shell themselves like nuts

For a purer green almond, our bare hands, O blind season.

SNOW

(Anne Hébert)

Snow puts us in a dream on vast plains without track or colour

Beware, my heart, snow puts us in the saddle on steeds of foam

Proclaim the coronation of childhood, snow consecrates us on high seas, dreams fulfilled, all sails set

Snow puts us in a trance, a widespread whiteness, flaring plumes pierced by the red eye of this bird

My heart; a point of fire under palms of frost flows the marvelling blood.

THE PRODIGAL SON

(Gilles Hénault, 1920-)

The child who used to play see him now thin and bowed
The child who used to weep see now his burnt-out eyes
The child who danced around see him running after a streetcar
The child who longed for the moon see him satisfied with a
     mouthful of bread
The wild and rebellious child, the child in the outskirts of the town
in the remote streets
The child of adventures
on the ice of the river
The child perched on fences
see him now in the narrow road of his daily routine
The child free and in play-clothes, see him now
disguised as a bill-board, a sandwich-man
dressed up in cardboard laws, a prisoner of petty taboos
subdued and trussed, see him hunted in the name of justice
The child of lovely red blood and of rich blood
see him now the ghost of a tragic opera

The prodigal child
The exceptional child
look at him now as a man
the man of "time is money" and the man of *bel canto*
the man riveted to his job which is to rivet all day
the man of Sunday afternoons in slippers
and the interminable bridge parties
the nameless man of the sports of the few men
and the man of the small bank account
to pay for the burial of a childhood that died
towards its fifteenth year.

HAIL TO THEE

(Gilles Hénault)

I

Redskins
Tribes consumed
in the conflagration of fire-water and tuberculosis
Hunted down by the pallor of death and the Palefaces
Carrying off your dreams of old spirits and the manitous
Dreams shattered by the fire of the arquebuses
You have left us your totemic hopes
And our sky now has the colour
of the smoke of your pipes of peace

II

We have no limits
And abundance is our mother
Land girdled with steel
With great lake eyes
And rustling resinous beard
I salute you and I salute your laughter of waterfalls
Land helmeted with polar ice
Haloed with northern lights
And offering to future generations
The sparkling sheaf of your uranium fires
We hurl against those who pillage and waste you
Against those who fatten upon your great body of humus and snow
The thunderous imprecations
That roar from the throats of storms

III

I already hear the song of those who sing:

Hail to thee, life, full of grace
the sower is with thee
blessed art thou by all women
and the child radiant with discovery
holds thee in his hand
like a multicoloured pebble of reality

Beautiful life, mother of our eyes
clothed in rain and sunny days
may thy kingdom come
on the roads and on the fields
Beautiful life
Praise be to love and to spring.

NOW COMES THE TIME

(Gilles Hénault)

I

I am one of those who accept
The light and the night of our lean years
I am one of those who read
The shadow of our hands on our future actions
I am one of those who speak
The mouth full of a bitter certainty
I am one of those who see
The sorcery of the world in the glances of women
I am one of those who comb
The tails of comets
I am one of those who know
That the miracle is in man
For I have gathered my loveliest flowers in the hoar-frost
Flowers of purest meaning
Where the light is caught in a trap.

II

Now comes the time of clear vision and new loveliness
After the hell of transformations.
The salt of the earth will cover the wounds of yesterday
Peace will pour its generous waters
On the ashes of our burnt hopes
The bloody harvest of men will no longer lean toward the mirror
    of the sky
And the devil's hide will dry in the four winds
Like a scarecrow.

LANDSCAPE ESTRANGED

(*Roland Giguère*, 1927-)

The storm raged about
and the snow blew into our breast
right in the breast
crowned with pain-sharp ice
crowned with thorns
love words driven into the brow

great storm before our eyes in a world estranged
every night tore a cry from us
and we grew up in agony
slowly we were aging
and the landscape aged with us   against us

the landscape was no longer the same
the landscape was sombre
the landscape no longer fitted us like a glove
no longer had the colours of our youth
the landscape the beautiful landscape was no longer beautiful
there were no more streams
no more ferns no water
there was nothing left

the landscape had to be remade.

POLAR SEASON

(*Roland Giguère*)

No flame. No warmth.
It was a cold life, the heart gripped in a ring of ice.

The sun had withdrawn its rays and finally left the humans who had insulted it for so long. They had spat in its face, in broad daylight; they had desecrated love like a whore, right on the street; they had dragged liberty through the mud and barbed wire. The noblest reasons for living torn to shreds under our windows and thrown to the four winds.

In autumn, we watched the dead leaves fall and, mentally, counted them among the green ones that we should not forget the colour of our hope. In our deepest selves, secretly and timidly, there still wavered the idea of the dignity of man.

But the centre of the earth was growing colder and colder. . . .

No flame. No warmth.
It was a cold life, the heart gripped in a ring of ice.

The eyes drained away, pierced by needles of cold. We that were brands became icicles, and everything froze in a terrible transparency.

White dominated, a cold white. A white that hid more than one festering wound of black, thick blood. But on the surface, to the eye, it was white. . . .

And the eye-sockets grew still, the flutter of eyelashes grew still, the beat of the wing grew still in a sky crystallized red and low while the other beating, of the heart, still kept on but now reached us deadened, muffled as though from far away, as though it moved farther and farther from the breast.

Those who continued to believe in something, no matter what, remained haggard. They were as lost as children in a railway station. They raved, adrift.

No flame. No warmth.
It was a cold life, the heart gripped in a ring of ice.

After death we would not rot but it would have been better to rot – to leave well-washed skeletons, clean remains, without a speck of flesh or blood, bones bleached and like new as the carcasses of horses that one finds on desert sands with skulls as beautiful as sculptures.

No, we would not rot but it would have been better to rot, for what was waiting for us was even worse: we were to be mummified at the foulest and most revolting moment of our lives and the image of our suffering preserved unchanged for ages and ages, reflected and magnified on the sky in humiliating auroras.

At any cost some other traces of ourselves had to be left, or none at all. None.

And we were there, caught in the ice, longing for a scorching summer.

No flame. No warmth.
It was a cold life, the heart gripped in a ring of ice.

And yet, a single night of universal love could save everything. A single white night of love and the earth is lighter; the sea withdraws into its bed taking with it the rags with which we are covered. Everything is washed clean. Man can sleep in white sheets without fear that his slumber may be murdered.

But at this time from which I speak to you, one saw even in the eyes of man a longing for man and it is in the eyes of animals that one found again the gentleness that makes you tear yourself from the ground and soar in the pure air, caught up in the ecstasy of the dream lived in flesh and bone. The flower, too, in spite of everything, clung to its petals, and after their migration the swallows came back to us as though there had always been a spring.

Silently, we sought a new horizon on which to find a foothold for a new life, to start all over again, to re-invent everything beginning with ourselves.

GREENER THAN NATURE

(*Roland Giguère*)

It's a time of prevailing breasts
in the fields of pleasure

the plundering hand takes its honey
from the heart of the original hive

the clover is bitter
and the sun has a face of wax

ANGEL

(Fernand Ouellette, 1930-)

The angel impregnated the stone

A long thread of silvery blood
flowed through the hardness of the landscape.
How the flowers all around
like elms wondered at growing!

And space, the impenetrable,
where the bird crashed
where the eye turned to stone,
in a shudder of the sky
split to its very soul.

COMMUNION

(Fernand Ouellette)

Naked, she wove herself into the ferns
her hair a glad welcome for butterflies.
I was her rich mould, her hidden nutriment
the musician of her strings.
I set her apart from the gold the green the transparency.
My life in her shone out from her very eyes.

TOWARDS DAWN

(*Fernand Ouellette*)

My body speaks to you takes you
burying itself in the moments of your flesh.
So worn so bloodless is your dream
so leprous my infinite agony
of the exhausted beast.

For I never stop dying
preying on the beautiful jade in your soul.

The more you give yourself
the more I graze my flocks on peak after peak
but the valleys drag me down.

How terrified I am when I hear the dawn
that prowls and attracts me wanting me changed.

But I block my ears.

I never stop wanting to die.

HOPE THAT TRIUMPHS

(Jean-Guy Pilon, 1930-)

Down below, in the most mysterious depths of space, the hand and its fingers emerge from the vast upheavals of the earth. Then the whole body sways upward on its twisted roots and calls to other bodies above the wreckage.

Suddenly, as the colour softens, the faces grow larger and lift up, and the eyes too and the hands and the men who take their place in this morning of too white a sun.

From that moment, man resumes his true stature above all things. He is king by his proud glance and lofty brow on which the beginnings of evil, like waves, roll in to die. Authority in order to live, and the patient strength of intelligence.

If one day you wander lost in these unfamiliar regions, and on the edge of the country where rocks crash together in the fury of the lightning you see a hand appear and thrust itself upward, you will be in the land of giants who are your brothers in the utmost way.

INVENTORY

(Jean-Guy Pilon)

I shall establish for you the inventory of my tenderness, the seasons which model my body and the whirling winds which hammer space.

What does it matter if the trumpets are shattered at the tolling from the ramparts, if encounters redden our earthen bed which we must acknowledge every night? No one shall share the secret of our abode.

Rings of thorn bushes may well overlie the roads that lead us into the city! We shall learn patience. Humbly. Our first steps will be sure and the footbridges that swayed yesterday will link the strangers and the besieged.

Because you will have placed between my latent cowardice and the triumph of our blood your profile of so few words, I shall know the strategy of beasts and the deep-laid plans of the wholly free tree.

THE STRANGER HEREABOUTS

(Jean-Guy Pilon)

He came from a country of devout pirates
Where indifference was taken for dogma
The idiot for the master
The sick man for the seer

It was a country of useless struggles
And magnificent ruins
A country eaten out by vermin

When he wished to shout out his rage
They would not allow it

They hardly allowed him to die

KNOWING

(*Jacques Brault*, 1933-)

I have in my mouth the honey of your mouth
   and of my body in your body
O strange country my beautiful stranger the name
   of this love that I do not know from your arms
around my neck like a night full of women
   regal in this strange country
No do not speak let the breath of your breath
   breathe on my lips
Do not speak stay with your moans wholly my sparrow
   my captive
And my silence is in your eyes like an unknown body
   I am absorbed in the water of your eyes
I am lost and search and roam in the kernel
   of your hair
I disappear in you O sleep of man O house of love
I die in you I have no face but your face and look
   you are grieving to die in me
You no longer exist I no longer exist   we are
   and as one come to our newness.

RUE SAINT-DENIS

(Jacques Brault)

The bells ring out on sullen Saint-Denis
    where I drag in the new year the thirtieth of my life
The bells ring out on sullen Saint-Denis
    and I am alone and naked like a little man-child in his bare skin
The bells ring out on sullen Saint-Denis
    and ruffle the pale surface of the sleeping griefs
The bells ring out on sullen Saint-Denis
    and quietly my tired memory covers itself
    with the linen shroud of the snow

I know that the shadows under the staircases
    laugh at my dreams
It will come soon that thing which happened
    only to another
It will come soon that thing which happens only
    to me
The cold light at the end of the street raises an
    arm and signals me

I think of this street of my childhood I think of
    winter among the grey houses
I hear the sound of another world in this street
    where my steps are ending
It was yesterday it is now the same cramped despair
    that limps along on the ice
The same clumsy and threadbare story at Julie's
    the forgetting days afterwards
I think of those faceless loves forgotten I don't know where

The bells ring out on sullen Saint-Denis
Their cracked voices repeat my sordid hours
The fumbling hand like a brute at the lap of the
    little girl
The jaundiced grass on the lawns the splash of
    shit on the sidewalk

The damp stale cigarette the six o'clock sun on the
  shoulder
The street that makes a noise like old black pennies
And in every show-case a chrome print of my pain

Beggar of my loves swindler of my own days
I'm going away yes I'm going away for good
I'm going away with one hand feeling the warmth of the other

The bells ring out on sullen Saint-Denis
And their dissonance wakens in me an old and a
  new gentleness
That thing at the end of the street is not so terrible
That thing that's come there to call me with its
  unseeing eye

STATE OF SIEGE

(*Pierre Trottier, 1925-*
For Gérard Pelletier

Fear of the police
Fear of arrests
Made me afraid of permissions
But even more of the unknown
And of the freedom that led to it

Fear of God
Fear of priests
Fear of men
And of the woman who gave them birth

Fear of my sins
Fear of confessing them
Made me afraid to receive grace
And the holiness that came with it

Fear of war
Fear of the enemy
Made me afraid of friends
And of the peace they heralded

Fear of words
Fear of thought
Made me afraid of magic formulas
And of the sorcerers who recited them

Sign of the cross or cry of race
Magic of amulet or mask
Oh the fear primitive the Indian fear
Which impelled me to work on the canoe of suicide

I had already carved a paddle of folksongs
The one that leads up there as high perhaps as the land
Where I might rejoin the *Chasse-Galerie*

354

But the minute I was ready
Authority had surrounded me
Had beamed its searchlights on me
Which relentlessly pinned me against the wall
Of the priestless prison of my conscience

À LA CLAIRE FONTAINE

(Pierre Trottier)

Let me bring you to the clear-running stream
Let me sing you the old songs

For a long time have I loved you
And never shall I forget you

Let me console your Cinderella people
Who cannot forget their Prince
And whose memories are but pale copies
Of a dream that faded and a hope too frail

For a long time have I loved you
And never shall I forget you

Let me console your poor school-children
Who only won prizes for remembrance
And who feel themselves prisoners of time
When they should take their place in history

For a long time have I loved you
And never shall I forget you

Let me bring you to the clear-running stream
Let me sing you the old songs

TIME CORRECTED

(Pierre Trottier)

So I retraced my steps
I retreated to my birth
And rolled back to their beginnings
My family and all my ancestors

I said a mass in reverse
That blood might taste of wine
That flesh might taste of bread
That I might return to the name of the Father
And never again say Amen

I returned everything I possessed
My faith to the King of Heaven
My tongue to the King of France
I gave back to Rome its hills
I dismissed the twelve Apostles
I sent home the shepherds and the Magi
I tore down Babel storey by storey
And returned the stone to the mountain
I sent back the dove to Noah
And drank all the waters of the Flood
I rehung the forbidden fruit on the tree
And handed to Satan the sin of knowledge
I took the first Eve again into my side
And restored sex to unity

And then
Nothing remained for me
But to give up the first sigh
In order to blow out the light
And everything returned to darkness

INDEX OF TITLES AND FIRST LINES

Note: Titles of poems, and titled sections of poems, are set in roman type. First lines of poems are in italic type. Wherever possible the date of composition is included with the individual title listing, and, where appropriate, the date of revision. The poems translated from French and Italian are similarly indexed by title and first line, but are grouped separately at the end of the index.

TRANSLATIONS

ACKNOWLEDGEMENTS

It was John Newlove who made a first draft of these Collected Poems and who, after some revision on my part, returned to edit the book in its final stages. To him my special thanks. Dr. Sandra Djwa added her invaluable critical judgements on various occasions. Professor Gary Geddes, then my colleague at Concordia University, took time from a busy schedule to read and criticize the collection. I relied heavily on the secretarial help generously given by Louise Parkin in sorting and keeping track of a mass of manuscript, as well as on her literary taste in the arrangement of the poems. As no single formula for selection seemed possible for the variety of interests that have dominated my writing during the past sixty years, I have divided the poems into categories within which the thematic and chronological relationships are generally followed.

Acknowledgements are due also to the following publishers and poets for permission to use translations from the French: *Editions Gallimard*, for Paul Eluard's "Vraie Justice," "Critique de la poésie" and "Avis" from *Poèmes pour tous*, Les Editeurs Français Réunis, 1959; *Les Editions de l'homme* for "The Philanthropists" of Jean Narrache from *"Quand j' parl' tout seul,"* Editions Albert Lévesque, 1932; *Les Editions du Noroît* for the two poems of Jacques Brault; *Les Editions Fides* for the poems of St.-Denys Garneau; Anne Hébert for her poems; *Editions Hexagone* and the poets themselves for the poems of Hénault, Giguère, Ouellette, Pilon, and Trottier.

F.R. Scott,
North Hatley, July 1981

NOTES

1. Section I "Indications," consists of a sampling of poems ranging roughly in date from the early 1920s to 1930. Some others of this period may appear in one of the other sections, fitting in because of the thematic arrangement of the rest of the book.

2. The italicized line in "Laurentian Shield" was taken from Stephen Spender's "How a Poem is Written"; and the italicized line in "Books of Poems" is the title of a book of poems by Dylan Thomas.